The Reading Terminal Market® Cookbook

SECOND EDITION

ANN HAZAN AND IRINA SMITH

CAMINO BOOKS, INC.

PHILADELPHIA

1 2 3 4   18 17 16 15

LIBRARY OF CONGRESS CATALOGING-IN-PUBLICATION DATA

Hazan, Ann, 1946-
The Reading Terminal Market cookbook / Ann Hazan and Irina Smith.
pages cm
Includes index.
ISBN 978-1-933822-92-1 (alk. paper)—ISBN 978-1-933822-93-8 (ebook)
1. Cooking, American. 2. Cooking—Pennsylvania—Philadelphia. 3. Reading
Terminal Market (Philadelphia, Pa.) I. Smith, Irina, 1942- II. Reading Terminal
Market (Philadelphia, Pa.) III. Title.

TX715.H3954 2015
641.59748'11—dc23   2014042740

Interior design: Rachel Reiss
Cover design: Jerilyn Bockorick

Reading Terminal Market is a registered trademark of Reading Company.
The trademark is used under license with permission of Reading Company.

This book is available at a special discount on bulk purchases
for promotional, business, and educational use.

Publisher
Camino Books, Inc
P.O. Box 59026
Philadelphia, PA 19102
www.caminobooks.com

With much love to our daughters,
Sophie Evelyn Moore,
Luisa Helena Gray
and Dorothy Ann Hazan,
with whom we have spent
many fun-filled and rewarding hours
at the Market.

———————

Contents

Foreword

Paul Steinke

FOR MORE THAN 300 YEARS, Philadelphia has stood as one of the great cities of America. Like all such cities, Philadelphia boasts fine parks, libraries, universities, museums, restaurants and the other trappings that make a city great. Yet our town can also boast of a major asset that many other American cities lack—a great public market. New York, Boston, Chicago and many other cities long ago let their public markets give way to urban decline and redevelopment.

Descended from colonial-era, open-air markets that once were strung down the middle of Market Street, Reading Terminal Market, in business since 1892, survived—but only barely—the waves of decline and renewal that swept over this city in the decades after World War II. Starting with a revival that began in the 1980s, Reading Terminal Market thrives today as Philadelphia's principal culinary jewel and primary cultural crossroads.

After more than 120 years, the Market serves a unique dual role: as a bountiful source of fresh foods and ingredients for home cooks, and as a must-see destination for authentic local color and cuisine for the city's ever-growing tourist trade. Filled daily with neighborhood shoppers, downtown office workers, tourists and conventioneers, the Market draws more than six million visitors per year.

In recent years, Reading Terminal Market has capitalized on the nationwide farm-to-table movement by showcasing its longstanding abundance of locally grown fruits and vegetables, while also recruiting new vendors who offer produce, meats and other products from farms within one or two hours' drive of the city. The result according to *Philadelphia Inquirer* food critic Craig LaBan, is "the region's best one-stop shop for a serious meal." Or as Michael Holahan, the founder and operator of the Market's Pennsylvania General Store, likes to put it, "You know the Market is thriving when dinner party hosts proudly proclaim that the meal was sourced from the Reading Terminal Market."

So as you begin to delve into the recipes that the Market's independent merchants have put forward in this wonderfully updated volume by Ann Hazan and Irina Smith, remember that a great public market is one of the attributes of a great city. And Philadelphia is fortunate to have the liveliest, most diverse and most delicious public market in the U.S.A.

Paul Steinke was General Manager of the Reading Terminal Market.

Thoughts on the Market

Cities build and plow under. Favorite haunts go dark. But the story of the Reading Terminal Market is that it is still with us, holding down the same acreage a century later. It has doubled down—a relic ripe with life, a memory still unburied, its story preciously rare and well worth telling... well.

—Rick Nichols, former food columnist for *The Philadelphia Inquirer*

The wondrous smells waft through the Market, putting people at ease. The presence of food defines the place as a huge tent under which hospitality and satisfaction can be expected.

—Professor Elijah Anderson, *The Cosmopolitan Canopy*

The Reading Terminal Market is full of amazing history, yet still relevant to the tastes of today's consumers. Not an easy feat!

—Paul Steinke, General Manager, Reading Terminal Market

The Reading Terminal Market is old yet new, constantly changing yet stable, local yet international. Truly incredible!

—Ann Hazan and Irina Smith, *The Reading Terminal Market Cookbook*

I've watched the incredible transformation of Philadelphia's culinary treasure, the Reading Terminal Market, from the early '70s, when it was at a low point with few vendors and too much empty space, to today, where it is a must-see destination for local, national and international food lovers. The Market is a place where everyone shops—rich, poor or in-between, where people from the myriad ethnic groups living in Philly can find the special ingredients they need, where local and seasonal produce abounds, and where there's always something new to try!

—Aliza Green, chef and author of *The Soupmaker's Kitchen* and *Making Artisan Pasta*

The Reading Terminal Market is a beloved Philadelphia institution, which not only provides access to fresh local food, but is a community gathering place that bridges cultures and brings collective joy to all who love the bustling aisles and colorful local character.

—Judy Wicks, author of *Good Morning, Beautiful Business* and founder of the White Dog Café

The Fair Food Farmstand was a new concept for the Reading Terminal Market back in 2003, and from day one, we were welcomed with open arms. Everyone from the maintenance and security staff, to the Market management, to the other vendors treated us like family and cheered us on as we grew from a "day staller" on an eight-foot table in center court to a full-time, year-round vendor. Yes, the Reading Terminal Market is our landlord, but we consider them a true partner in our business.

—Ann Karlen, Executive Director, Fair Food Farmstand

The Reading Terminal Market has remained an iconic part of the historical fabric of Philadelphia. It is a social hub for Center City and one of the most popular places downtown for dining, shopping, events and, of course, people-watching.

—Carol Rhea, President, American Planning Association

Acknowledgments

WE TRULY LOVE THE MARKET AND ITS PEOPLE. Writing the first *Reading Terminal Market Cookbook* was memorable. Writing this new edition was incredibly inspiring yet bittersweet, with the departure of some of the founding Market families and longtime merchants. The Market is as dynamic as ever with new, exciting vendors and another generation following their family traditions. We couldn't have done this alone without the cooperation and help of others. We wish especially to thank:

The merchants of the Market—who endured our endless quest for information and who spent many hours talking with us. Thanks also for your faith in the Market throughout the years and for sharing your recipes and wonderful stories.

The Market customers—who allowed all of us to enjoy your treasured recipes. Thanks for your loyalty and support in keeping the Market alive and active for the people of the city.

Edward Jutkowitz, our publisher—who had the vision, as we did, to see the importance of keeping the Reading Terminal Market and its history alive through this cookbook. Thank you for your continued interest in working with us through four cookbooks.

Brad Fisher, Senior Editor at Camino Books—we enjoyed working with you on this new edition, just as we did on the first.

Paul Steinke, former General Manager—who deserves a huge round of applause for bringing the Market into a new era. We also thank you for sharing your extensive knowledge of the Market's history.

Sarah Levitsky, Marketing and Special Events Coordinator—who was always willing and able to answer our questions and help out. You are great at what you do.

Rick Nichols, former food columnist for *The Philadelphia Inquirer*—who contributed enthusiasm and passion and who supported the Market over the years. The articles in The Rick Nichols Room in the Market are a wealth of information. Thank you for sharing so much with all of us.

Herb Hazan and Angus Smith, our husbands—who willingly offered to taste the recipes and who were always patient and encouraging.

Dorothy Hazan, Ann's daughter—who read every page of every chapter. Your gift for the written word helped us immensely, and what fun we had!

Introduction

PHILADELPHIA'S READING TERMINAL MARKET opened its doors on February 22, 1892, and it was quickly recognized as one of the world's great food emporiums. More than a century later, it still is.

Reading Terminal Market is a traditional stall market. Its approximately 80 merchants represent a wide variety of ethnic backgrounds and Philadelphia neighborhoods. Some of the merchants sell meats, poultry, fish, produce, groceries, honey, nuts, specialty oils, vinegars and chocolates, while others sell prepared foods to eat in or take out. There are bakeries as well as beverage, dairy and cheese stalls. Where else can you find a Syrian immigrant frying falafel, a Korean artistically arranging fruits and vegetables, a Pennsylvania Dutch farmer displaying a traditional favorite like shoofly pie, women in pinafores with traditional white head caps rolling and twisting the ever-popular soft pretzel, and an African American at a Sicilian sandwich stand slicing prosciutto—all under one roof?

Today, Reading Terminal Market attracts over 100,000 customers a week and is the food destination of choice for Philadelphians who live and work in the city, as well as for many suburbanites. It's situated in Center City at 12th and Arch Streets—close to trains, buses, downtown department stores, hotels, offices and the city's Chinatown. In 1994, the Market got a new neighbor: the mammoth Pennsylvania Convention Center across Arch Street. Almost overnight, the Market's customer base grew dramatically, with conventioneers and out-of-towners joining the locals at this splendidly preserved site, a tremendous resource that is listed in the National Register of Historic Places.

David Bassett having lunch with friends in the Rick Nichols Room.

The Shoe Doctor.

Hundreds flock to the Market to enjoy breakfast, lunch or an early dinner. At lunchtime especially, the counters and seating areas fill up with hungry patrons from all walks of life. At midday, there are often free musical performances at the Market: piano, jazz, soft rock and more by locals, including judges, architects and surgeons.

The Market is renowned for its Amish and Mennonite farmers and merchants, many of whom come from Lancaster County. Indeed, the Market is well known for its many regional specialties. The Reading Terminal Market was voted the Best of Philly tourist attraction in 2013. Since 1973, the Market and its merchants have been named Best of Philly 85 times. In 2012, Philadelphia was one of only six cities nationwide selected to host an event—"Summer Eats," an extravaganza of summer picnic foods—by the Cooking Channel. In 2014, the Market was chosen by the American Planning Association as one of the 10 Great Public Places in America. It was even featured in a scene from the 2004 adventure movie, *National Treasure*.

In addition to being a food emporium, the Market boasts a cookware shop, a French linen shop, a well-stocked cookbook stall, a demonstration and culinary events kitchen, a wine shop, several craft shops featuring the clothing and jewelry of local artisans, a flower shop, The Rick Nichols Room, a community room for special events, and even a shoeshine stand.

The Market's history goes back to the original open-air markets set up on the banks of the Delaware River in the late 1600s. These markets later moved to an arcade in the center of what was then known as High Street (now Market Street). As the city developed, these markets extended farther west, to the area between 11th and 12th Streets. In 1859, the open-air street markets closed and were replaced by a market house known as Farmers' Market, which was joined a few years later by the adjacent Franklin Market.

When the Reading Railroad was looking for a site for its proposed Reading Terminal, it negotiated for the site of the markets by offering to build merchants a new indoor facility as part of the train complex. The railroad built the train shed, a grand head-house at 12th and Market Streets, as well as a food market that was unrivaled in America.

Reading Terminal Market became the center for food distribution for the city. Foods could now easily be shipped in by train. Beneath the market floor was a massive cold-storage area—about 500,000 cubic feet of space divided into rooms of varying temperatures for properly storing different meats, poultry, fruits and vegetables. The Market also provided ice to merchants and for the railroad's passenger cars, dining facilities and refrigerated express cars.

Many of the longstanding Market merchants remember being told how the carriages of the wealthy would line up on 12th Street while the chefs shopped for their employers. These same merchants also recalled the hard times—the two world wars, the Depression, food rationing and food stamps. They remembered the impact of these events on themselves, as well as on their families, businesses and customers.

Those were the days when the Market effectively served the needs of Philadelphians. But after World War II, it suffered a decline as mass-marketing, fast food and suburbanization took an ever-greater hold in America. Food began to move by truck as more highways were built, and Reading Terminal Market's own food network began to deteriorate, as did the Market's structure and appearance. By the 1970s, it was in serious trouble and was showing signs of ruin and decay. By the time the last train rolled out of Reading Terminal in the 1980s, the Market's fortunes were looking bleak.

To help stimulate business in the early '80s, the Reading Company made major renovations and worked to increase the numbers of eat-in and take-out food stands. David O'Neil, who became the Market's general manager in 1981, played a pivotal role in its resurgence. In addition to recruiting new eateries and other interesting merchants, he went out to Lancaster County, an hour's drive but a world away, and persuaded many Amish and Mennonite farmers to establish a Pennsylvania Dutch section. It would become one of the Market's major attractions. Some of the vendors would sell not just prepared foods, but the ingredients for their specialties.

O'Neil was sustained partly by his own boyhood experiences at the Market and his growing love for the place: "It's a throwback where people used to fast food can experience what it was like before America was gobbled up by chains. Here you can get the ethnic diversity of Philadelphia and all the neighborhoods. You come here and people say, 'Hi, how are you?' You know the meat man. I think in a city, people really crave human contact—and they get it at the Market."

Many of the founding merchants stayed on during the tough times, remaining loyal to Reading Terminal Market and nurturing faith that it would return to its grander days. The Market was, in fact, coming back.

Its brush with disaster might explain the fear that surrounded the next critical period in the Reading Terminal Market's tumultuous history. The planning and construction of a convention center across the way on Arch Street had merchants and shoppers fearing for the Market's survival as a true farmers market. Locals

A Pennsylvania Dutch baker with her wares.

feared a change in the nature of the merchants. Would the Market become a "souvenir trap"? Would it discourage and turn off loyal customers? Or would it be torn down and destroyed altogether as a huge convention center went up? "Save the Market" buttons began popping up everywhere, and thousands signed petitions urging the preservation of this city treasure.

Their fears did not materialize. Change did occur, but the Market held on. Despite considerable acrimony, the Reading Terminal Market Merchants' Association worked things out with the Pennsylvania Convention Center Authority. The Reading Railroad had supported the Market in the 1890s, and now the Convention Center Authority would support it in the 1990s. Renovations were desperately needed, and they were made, though not without great pain to the merchants and shoppers. During this period, one section of the Market at a time was closed off, and merchants had to endure temporary relocation. But the site remained open. When it was done, the structure and its supporting electrical, plumbing and air-conditioning systems were improved, and it got the new roof it so badly needed. The Market was cleaner, brighter and cooler in the summer. Once again, it had been thrown into turmoil, and once again, it survived.

The not-for-profit Reading Terminal Market Corporation assumed management responsibility in September 1995 with a 30-year lease and a mission to preserve the historic Market as a shopping destination for the widest range of locally grown and produced food. Marcene Rogovin, who took over as the Market's general manager, commented, "It remained the one place where people from every neighborhood and different backgrounds could come together to promote rural-urban links and to highlight the culture and heritage of the region's farming community."

Two major organizations were established to strengthen the Market's influence in the community. The Reading Terminal Farmers' Market Trust was created by Market merchants in 1991 to support stable sources of fresh, affordable, quality foods in underserved communities and to strengthen the connection between farmers and consumers. The Trust is a charitable organization that operates in local farmers' markets in partnership with communities throughout the city. In 1993, the Reading Terminal Market Merchants' Catering Company was formed, utilizing all the merchants and their specialties to cater evening events and private parties, large and small.

Paul Steinke, a native Philadelphian who is eternally proud of his hometown, took the reins of the Reading Terminal Market as general manager in October 2001. The Market was about to enter into another phase, one that would take it to even greater heights. Paul works with merchants, staff and a board of directors to uphold and strengthen the Market's mission to "preserve the architectural and historical character, and function, of the Reading Terminal Market as an urban farmers' market." Among his achievements, he initiated a new and simplified customer parking program in 2004, introduced regular Sunday hours for the first time in the Market's history in 2006, and launched a Market-wide gift card program in 2012. Paul has also recruited dozens of locally based, independent merchants who have greatly expanded and enhanced the Market's cultural and culinary appeal. Examples include a local foods farm stand; local producers of honey, cheese, wine and humanely raised lamb; a Jewish deli and a from-scratch bakery; and Cajun, German, Indo-Pakistani and soul food stands, among many others. In 2011 and '12, Paul Steinke oversaw the design, financing and construction of a $3.5 million improvement project that built new and expanded rest rooms, a new demonstration kitchen and community room, new refrigerated merchant storage and additional space for a half-dozen new merchant stores. During Paul's tenure, annual visits to the Market have increased from 4.8 million in 2002 to more than 6.2 million visitors per year today.

Many of the longtime merchants are still around; some have relocated to larger spaces, while a few are but fond memories. The longtime customers, however, are still frequenting their favorite shopping and eating places, and the Market continues to serve the community and the region in its historic setting.

Farmers' markets in this country have taken on a new ambiance. Homegrown produce and organic farming have gained increasing popularity and respect. Although farmers' markets are not new to the Philadelphia region or, for that matter, to the world, fresh foods have become very important to Americans, and markets have adapted to the trend. These are the places where you can find seasonal products, homemade vinegars, home-baked breads and local honeys, and where you know the farmer or producer by name. It has become a way of life for many people, one that the Reading Terminal Market has adopted.

Mastering the intricacies of selling in farmers' markets around the world can be fascinating, challenging and, at times, frustrating. Most merchants are proud of what they do and often display a refined sense of artistry. They painstakingly arrange fruits and vegetables in attractive, orderly displays, and the butchers and

Laura DiFrancesco, proprietor of Contessa's French Linens,
specializing in table cloths and napkins from Provence.

poulterers will often take time to describe a certain cut of meat or give out recipes for preparation.

For centuries, markets in Philadelphia have provided an incentive for cooking with their access to fresh ingredients and compelling environment. Another Philadelphia attraction—and in some respects a competitor of the Reading Terminal Market—is the historic Italian Market, located on 9th Street in South Philadelphia. There are farmers' and public markets across the nation, including New York's Union Square Market, the Fulton Fish Market and the Bronx Terminal Market; Baltimore's Lexington Market and Broadway Market; and Seattle's Pike Place Market. There are renowned food markets in Paris, London, Venice and Prague, as well as in Hong Kong, Beijing, Delhi and Mumbai, all offering unique foods and unforgettable cultural experiences. Luckily, you don't have to travel thousands of miles. Philadelphia's Reading Terminal Market catches the essence of many flavors from around the world and is considered by many to be the best market in the United States.

We can attest to Reading Terminal Market's outstanding qualities because, for more than 35 years, we have enjoyed it and basked in what it has to offer. Shop-

Linens, gifts and kitchen basics from Amy's Place.

ping and spending time in farmers' markets was not a new experience for us. As youngsters, our parents would take us along to the neighborhood markets wherever we lived at the time. And as we grew older and traveled on our own to even more cities around the world, we were still drawn to the markets, out of curiosity and interest. Many of the markets were charming in their own right, and we were pleased to see them bustling with activity. But we both agreed that there was no place like home, meaning our very own Reading Terminal Market. It is truly our second home, especially after years of researching and writing this cookbook, which we hope is a tribute to its greatness. We especially love chatting with the merchants and customers. The Market atmosphere lends itself to really getting to know its people, the people we call the Market family.

We enjoyed hearing the story from one loyal customer who recalled how she came to shop at the Market. One day, her cat ate the veal chop that her mother-in-law had put out for dinner, so she went to the Market to buy another chop. The woman who waited on her was so bubbly and friendly that the customer ended up telling her the circumstances of her purchase. They both had a good laugh. The customer was so impressed with how accommodating the merchant was that she went back time and time again. We love the story, for we believe it captures the warmth of the Market, the friendly, more-than-willing-to-help-you place to shop.

Reading Terminal Market is never more alive and wonderful than during the holiday seasons. We can't wait for each new season to arrive with its bounty of holiday foods and seasonal fruits and vegetables. Every year we look forward to seeing customers select their turkey or duck for holiday dinner and delighting in the stalls' festive decorations. When we see the first pussy willows and tulips at the flower stand, we know that spring is just around the corner, and soon we'll be able to feast on crabs and homegrown corn all summer long.

The Market features many special annual events throughout the year, such as the Pennsylvania Dutch Festival, Scrapple Fest, the Side Walk Sizzle and Ice Cream Freeze, the Harvest Festival and the Festival of Forgotten Foods Day, to name but a few. A popular Philadelphia tradition, the Valentine to the Market fundraiser is back and better than ever. All are of these events are well attended by thousands of people who eagerly anticipate them every year.

Many of the Market's events and celebrations now take place in The Rick Nichols Room, a community space honoring the longtime *Inquirer* journalist who has been a strong champion of the Market. Nichols was instrumental in keeping the Market open during its dark days; he celebrated its revival and believed in its future.

If you enter from the 12th and Filbert Street entrance, you'll find a green desk with a big information sign on top. Sitting behind that desk will be a volunteer eager to help you navigate the Market, give you a map and answer your questions, whether they are Market-related or about Philadelphia and its surroundings. If you're in the mood for a particular food or looking for a special ingredient, you'll get assistance with a smile. Many volunteers have served for years and are very knowledgeable. They have different life experiences, but what they all have in common is a love for this gem of a place. The information center has been renamed for Becky Stoloff, a longtime Market Corporation and Preservation Fund board member.

Philbert the Pig, the huge bronze piggy bank sculpted by Eric Berg and found in the center court at the Market, has been a popular meeting spot for local customers and visitors alike. His name is a play on the Market's Filbert street entrance. Philbert receives coins from generous customers, and the proceeds go to various charitable causes.

Over the years, we have conducted cooking classes at the Market, and we've introduced many of our students and tourists to what it has to offer. The Market is a place where we bring our friends and family to spend some of the most enjoyable times together. Whether we stay to eat or shop for food to prepare at home, we feel we are getting the best there is.

This cookbook is a celebration of Reading Terminal Market and is meant to open your eyes to a great Philadelphia tradition. Customers who live in the city enjoy walking to the Market to shop and to talk with their many merchant friends. The Market also offers access to virtually all of the area's mass transportation, so people who live outside Center City can shop in their favorite place as well. Business people enjoy taking a break and lunching at their favorite counter. Every day, conventioneers are discovering this exciting bazaar of new and old merchants, and browsing tourists are surprised at the liveliness of this turn-of-the-century landmark. The aisles, laid out as alleys and avenues, give one the feeling of strolling down neighborhood streets within the small world of a marketplace.

More than simply guiding you through this remarkable place, we hope that this book will introduce you to a new way of enjoying a Saturday morning or a weekday lunch break, or that brief respite before the train ride home when you can select your favorite prepared dish or the ingredients for a special dinner. This cookbook includes contributions from recent and longtime merchants, as well as from those who were part of the original Market family. We may not see their stands anymore, but many people still remember them fondly with even a favorite

The famous statue of Philbert the Pig in the Market's center court.

story or two. This book includes recipes from Market merchants for foods available at their stands; some are treasured family recipes, while others make use of the vast selection of ingredients available at the Market. Finally, we have added some of our favorite recipes. As you can guess, we make these from foods we buy at our favorite source. We know that you will delight, as we have, in the diversity and timeless grace of Philadelphia's Reading Terminal Market.

Bakery
Merchants

PHILADELPHIANS HAVE LONG had a deep love affair with good breads and a passion for pastries. Reading Terminal Market has the best of both. Some of the bakeries now in the Market began their businesses in other parts of the city and then expanded to include Market locations—much to the delight of the owners, who saw immediate success, and the Market customers, who had always been loyal to local products. Reading Terminal Market is now home to some of the best bakeshops in the city.

The story of the Famous 4th Street Cookie Company began at the 4th Street Deli, then owned by David Auspitz. For years, the deli sold only one brand of ice cream, but when Auspitz started carrying another brand, the first manufacturer ripped out the freezer, leaving a large hole. David's wife, Janie, wanted to use the space to sell her cookies. They had become a Philadelphia favorite. Reading Terminal Market has enjoyed the results. Famous 4th Street Cookie Company carries over 12 varieties of cookies. They are especially known for their black-and-white and chocolate-dipped double chocolate chip cookies. But do not miss trying the oatmeal raisin and snickerdoodle cookies.

Flying Monkey Bakery, owned and operated by Elizabeth Halen, opened in October 2010 and quickly became a favorite. They make each and every element of each and every sweet right at the Market each and every day. They are known for Pumpple Cake—the infamous pies baked inside of cakes—as well as more humble treats such as buttercakes and "whoopie" pies. Their signature Elvis Cake is available by special order and pairs a rich peanut butter buttercream frosting with a moist banana chocolate chip cake. Their handcrafted baked goods, confections and cakes are made with only the finest ingredients and a touch of whimsy.

Market Bakery, owned by Roger Bassett, is one of the few places in the Market to supply just about every bread and pastry need, from artisan varieties like their sun-dried tomato bread to classics like rye, Italian and multigrain. Market Bakery is filled with all sorts of breads and pastries, most from Philadelphia's Le Bus bakery and other local artisan bakers. They also have sandwiches made on their fabulous breads. For breakfast, try the bacon, turkey, ham and sausage sandwich, and at lunchtime, be sure to try their fresh-baked focaccia and their Baguette Melt, made to order.

Be warned. As you wait in line at Metropolitan Bakery, your order will swell with each item you see—from just-baked sourdough baguettes to hand-shaped, all-natural loaves to intricate seasonal pastries. And it's almost impossible to resist their addictive granola, called "best in the nation" by Epicurious.com, or their lauded sour cherry chocolate chip cookies, which *The Philadelphia Inquirer* calls "one of the all-time greatest." When Wendy Smith Born and chef James Barrett opened the doors of the Metropolitan Bakery in November 1993, they gave Philadelphians something they didn't know they couldn't live without: breads and pastries made in the Old World style, with all-natural ingredients, a slow-fed sourdough starter, a "long-slow-cool" rise and crackling crusts. Since then, the bakery has grown to include breakfast treats, rolls, pizzas, desserts and pastries, specialty items, coffee, 30 varieties of bread and, in 2013, a sit-down café in Rittenhouse Square. Now, thanks to their new online shop, Metropolitan Bakery items are available nationwide.

Termini Brothers Bakery, a family-owned business since 1921, was founded by Giuseppe Termini, and is one of Philadelphia's best-known and oldest Italian bakeries. Owner Vincent Termini opened his business in the Market in 1984. Now his two sons, Joseph, a Saint Joseph's University food marketing graduate, and Vincent Jr., a Culinary Institute of America graduate, are following the family tradition. All the authentic Italian pastries are prepared in Termini's flagship store located near South Philadelphia's Italian Market. Termini's ships tinned, handmade Italian cookies and their famous cannolis nationwide. "The cannolis are shipped by packing the shell separately from the filling, which is cooler-packed," explains Vincent. This method preserves the crispness of the shell, which anyone who has tasted a Termini cannoli can attest to. The store offers cannolis, biscotti, cakes and cookies, all displayed behind cases that seem to stretch on forever.

Check the Pennsylvania Dutch section of the Market and in this book for additional bakeries and recipes.

Past Merchants of the Market

Braverman's Bakery, owned by Gene and Rosalyn Braverman, was a part of the Market for many years until their closing in 2005. They were best known for their internationally inspired selections: French truffles, Italian tiramisu, German linzer tortes and strudels as well as Russian rugalach and black bread.

Although David Braverman's Le Bus bakery no longer has a stand in the Market, their wonderful artisan breads and pastries are still available at the Market Bakery.

Old Post Road is another fondly remembered stand. On Fridays and Saturdays, Hans Stulz would be found setting up freshly baked cakes and pies that his wife, Claudia, helped prepare and bake.

The wonderful recipes of the Bravermans and the Stulzes are still featured in this new edition.

Ann Hazan's Pumpkin Bread Pudding

This is a wonderful bread pudding for all seasons. In winter, I serve it with whipped cream and, when the weather is warmer, with vanilla ice cream—from Bassetts Ice Cream, of course!

⅔ cup golden raisins
¼ cup bourbon or rum
5 cups cranberry or cinnamon
    bread, cut into ½-inch cubes
2 cups half and half
3 large eggs
⅔ cup granulated sugar
⅔ cup packed light brown sugar

1 15-ounce can solid pack pumpkin
3 tablespoons unsalted butter,
    melted
2 teaspoons pumpkin pie spice
1 teaspoon pure vanilla extract
½ cup semisweet chocolate chips
Whipped cream or vanilla ice
    cream, optional

Preheat oven to 350 degrees.

Butter a 12 × 8 × 2-inch baking pan.

In a bowl, combine raisins and bourbon (or rum), set aside.

Place bread cubes in a bowl. Pour half and half over bread and set aside.

In another bowl, combine eggs, sugars, pumpkin, melted butter, pumpkin pie spice and vanilla. Stir until well blended. Combine with soaked bread cubes. Add reserved raisins and chocolate chips. Stir to combine.

Pour mixture into prepared pan and bake approximately 45 minutes or until custard is just set. Serve warm or cold with whipped cream or ice cream, if desired.

Makes six to eight servings

Bittersweet Chocolate Chip Cookies with Sea Salt and Dried Cherries

Metropolitan Bakery provided this delicious recipe for all our chocolate chip cookie cravings. Combining bittersweet chocolate chunks and dried tart cherries creates a perfect pairing. The little sprinkling of coarse sea salt on top gives them a sweet/salty flavor that is irresistible.

1 cup rolled oats
3 cups all-purpose flour
1¾ teaspoons baking powder
1½ teaspoons baking soda
1¼ teaspoons kosher salt
¾ pound (3 sticks) unsalted butter
1¼ cups granulated sugar

1¾ cups light brown sugar
3 large eggs
1½ teaspoons pure vanilla extract
1½ cups extra bittersweet chocolate
   chips
1¼ cups dried tart cherries
Coarse sea salt for sprinkling

In the bowl of a food processor, grind oats until fine.

In a bowl, sift flour with baking powder and baking soda. Add kosher salt and finely ground oats. Set aside.

In the bowl of an electric mixer fitted with a paddle attachment, cream butter and sugars together until light, approximately 3 minutes. Add eggs, one at a time. Stir in vanilla. Add reserved flour mixture and mix until just combined. Fold in chocolate chips and cherries.

With an ice cream scoop, portion cookie dough into 4-ounce balls. Place cookies on a parchment-lined tray. Wrap and chill overnight, or up to 3 days.

Preheat oven to 350 degrees.

Place cookies on two baking sheets, 2 inches apart. Press slightly to flatten and sprinkle each cookie with ¼ teaspoon coarse sea salt. Bake 15 to 18 minutes, rotating the baking sheets between the upper and lower oven racks halfway through baking until cookies are golden brown around the edges. Transfer cookies to wire racks to cool completely or serve warm (if you can't wait).

Makes one and a half dozen cookies

Chocolate Chip Biscotti with Almonds

This recipe is from the Braverman family who once owned the highly regarded Braverman's Bakery in the Market. Rosalyn Braverman and daughter Diane, after much trial and error, finally put together this biscotti recipe that pleased not only them, but friends and relatives, too. "These chocolate almond biscotti go terrifically with a cup of espresso, cappuccino or hot chocolate," Diane Braverman commented, "and not so well dipped in wine as are the ones made with only ground almonds." She was referring to the Italian tradition of dipping plain biscotti into dry red wine.

2 cups unbleached flour
½ teaspoon baking powder
½ teaspoon salt
1 cup minus 1 tablespoon sugar
7 ounces whole almonds, with or without skins

12 ounces semisweet chocolate chips
2 large eggs
1 teaspoon vanilla extract
1 tablespoon almond-flavored liqueur

Position the two oven racks so that the oven is divided into three equal sections.

Line cookie sheets with parchment paper or foil with shiny side up.

Preheat oven to 375 degrees.

In a large bowl, sift together the flour, baking powder and salt. Stir in the sugar.

In the work bowl of a food processor, add ½ cup of the flour mixture and ½ cup of the almonds, and process for 30 seconds, or until a light powder forms. Combine this mixture with the rest of the sifted ingredients, then coarsely chop the remaining nuts and add them to the sifted ingredients along with the chocolate chips.

In another small bowl, beat the eggs with vanilla and the liqueur just enough to mix. Add this mixture to the dry ingredients, stirring to moisten them. Do not overmix.

Working with wet hands and on a large sheet of parchment or wax paper, shape the dough into a long mound. Cut dough into quarters, and, keeping your hands wet, shape each quarter of dough into strips about 10 inches long, 2½ inches wide, and ¾ inch high. (Use only your hands, not a rolling pin.) Place dough on the prepared trays, and place the trays on the racks in the oven. Bake for approximately 20 minutes. Midway through the baking, switch the top and bottom trays and rotate front to back.

Remove from oven, slide parchment off the trays, and using a wide metal spatula, place biscotti on a cutting board. Let cool for 10 to 15 minutes. Reduce oven temperature to 275 degrees. With a serrated knife, cut at a 45-degree angle into ½-inch-wide slices. Cut slowly, using a sawing motion. Place slices cut side down on the two cookie sheets, this time without a lining. Return to oven, and bake for 20 to 25 minutes, again switching trays top and bottom and front to back once. Carefully turn slices (they'll be hot). Turn oven off and leave biscotti in oven to cool, then store in sealed container.

Makes 40 pieces

Cornbread Loaf

This recipe is from Le Bus bakery, once located in the Reading Terminal Market. Market Bakery now occupies that location and continues to carry a selection of Le Bus products. Le Bus started near the University of Pennsylvania, and baked their first loaf of bread in a small propane oven inside a converted school bus. This recipe appeared in our first *Reading Terminal Market Cookbook*.

1½ cups all-purpose flour
1½ cups yellow cornmeal, more for
   dusting
½ cup sugar
½ teaspoon baking powder
½ teaspoon baking soda
½ teaspoon salt

2 large eggs
½ cup vegetable oil
½ cup milk
½ cup buttermilk
1 cup corn kernels, fresh or frozen
   (thawed)

Preheat oven to 350 degrees.

Grease a 9 × 5-inch loaf pan, dust with cornmeal and shake off excess.

In a large bowl, combine flour, cornmeal, sugar, baking powder, baking soda and salt. In a medium bowl, whisk eggs, oil, milk and buttermilk. Add egg mixture and the corn to the dry ingredients and stir just until combined. Do not overmix. Pour batter into prepared pan and bake for 15 minutes. Reduce temperature to 325 degrees and bake about 1 hour longer or until a tester inserted into center of loaf comes out clean.

Cool bread in pan on a rack for 30 minutes. Turn out onto rack. Serve warm or at room temperature.

Makes one loaf, about six servings

Elvis Cake

This recipe comes from the Flying Monkey Bakery and is based on one of Elvis' favorites—the peanut butter and banana sandwich. Originally, it was called "hunk of burning love cake," but was changed to make it more approachable.

CAKE
2 cups all-purpose flour
1 cup cake flour
1 tablespoon baking powder
¼ pound (1 stick) unsalted butter, softened to room temperature
2 cups granulated sugar
2 teaspoons kosher salt
3 large eggs
2 cups buttermilk, well shaken
1 tablespoon vanilla extract
2 ripe bananas, mashed

1 cup mini chocolate chips (reserve ⅓ cup for garnish)

PEANUT BUTTER FROSTING
½ pound (2 sticks) unsalted butter, room temperature
1 cup creamy peanut butter
4 cups powdered sugar
2 tablespoons milk, additional if necessary for spreading consistency

Preheat oven to 350 degrees.

Grease and flour two 9-inch round cake pans.

In a bowl, mix together the flours and baking powder and set aside.

In a large bowl, cream butter, sugar and salt until light and fluffy. Add eggs one at a time, beating thoroughly after each addition. Add flour mixture alternately with buttermilk, beating just to combine. Finally, stir in vanilla and mashed bananas. Pour batter evenly into prepared pans. Sprinkle each cake with ⅓ cup of the mini chocolate chips and bake for 35 minutes, or until a toothpick inserted into the cake comes out clean. Cool cake layers completely, turn out of pans and frost. Garnish with remaining chocolate chips.

To make frosting, with an electric mixer, cream together butter and peanut butter until smooth and fully incorporated. Add powdered sugar a cup at a time and use milk to adjust the consistency for easy spreading.

Makes 10 to 12 servings, or for one "King"

Focaccia

This interesting and delicious version of focaccia from Roger Bassett of Market Bakery is sure to become a favorite in your home. The Kalamata olive and Parmesan cheese toppings give it a distinctive twist.

2 teaspoons rapid-rising dry yeast
1 cup warm water
2 tablespoons sugar
3½ to 4 cups all-purpose flour
1 tablespoon coarse salt
¼ cup olive oil
Cornmeal for dusting

TOPPING
2 tablespoons olive oil
1 onion, diced
2 garlic cloves, minced
10 Kalamata olives, pitted and
    quartered
¼ cup shredded Parmesan cheese
1 tablespoon coarse salt
Freshly ground black pepper to
    taste
2 tablespoons fresh rosemary

In the bowl of a standing mixer fitted with a dough hook, proof the yeast by combining it with the warm water and sugar. Stir gently to dissolve. Let stand 3 minutes until foam appears. Turn mixer on low and slowly add the flour to the bowl. Dissolve salt in 2 tablespoons of water and add it to the mixture. Pour in ¼ cup olive oil. When dough begins to come together, increase mixer speed to medium and continue beating. Stop the machine periodically to scrape dough off the hook. Mix until the dough is smooth and elastic, about 10 minutes, adding flour as necessary.

Turn dough out onto a work surface and fold over a few times. Form the dough into a round and place in an oiled bowl. Turn to coat the entire ball with oil so it doesn't form a skin. Cover with plastic wrap or damp towel and let rise over a gas pilot light on the stovetop or other warm place until doubled in size, about 45 minutes.

Coat a sheet pan with a little olive oil and cornmeal. Once the dough is doubled and domed, turn it out onto the counter. Roll and stretch the dough out to an oblong shape about ½-inch thick. Lay the flattened dough on the pan and cover with plastic wrap. Let rest for 15 minutes.

Preheat oven to 400 degrees.

While dough is resting, make topping. Coat a small sauté pan with olive oil, add the onion and cook over low heat for 15 minutes until the onions caramelize. Uncover the dough and dimple with your fingertips. Brush the surface with more olive oil and then add caramelized onions, garlic, olives, cheese, salt, pepper and rosemary. Bake on the bottom rack for 15 to 20 minutes.

Makes one focaccia

Assorted breads from the Market Bakery.

German Apple Cake

Old Post Road—once a bakery stand at the Market on Fridays and Saturdays—was popular for the cakes and pies featured by Hans Stulz, prepared and baked by his wife, Claudia. Hans suggested using a tart apple for this cake. This recipe appeared in our first Market cookbook.

¼ pound (1 stick) butter, softened
½ cup sugar
2 teaspoons vanilla
1 teaspoon lemon extract
3 large eggs
1¾ cups all-purpose flour
2 teaspoons baking powder

5 to 6 Rome or Granny Smith
    apples depending on size, peeled,
    cored and halved
2 tablespoons apricot jam
1 tablespoon water
Whipped cream, optional

Preheat oven to 350 degrees.

In a bowl, cream the butter and sugar until well blended. Add vanilla and lemon extracts. Beat in the eggs, one at a time. Sift together the flour and baking powder and add to the batter. Mix until well blended. The batter will be stiff. Spoon batter into a 10-inch springform pan and, using the back of a spoon or spatula, spread it evenly over the entire bottom of the pan.

Cut each apple half into 6 to 8 slices. Starting in the middle of the batter, place the apple slices in concentric circles until the pan is full. Bake for 35 to 45 minutes, or until a cake tester inserted in the middle comes out dry.

Meanwhile, place the apricot jam and water in a small saucepan, and, over low heat, cook until the jam liquifies. Stir until smooth.

When cake is done, let cool for 10 to 15 minutes. Remove from the springform pan, and brush top with the apricot mixture. Serve warm or at room temperature with whipped cream, if desired.

Makes six servings

Market Customer: Betty Kaplan

Betty Kaplan has worked at the Market in various capacities including conducting tours. She found the original recipe for a pepper apple pie attached to a jar of green peppercorns. Intrigued by the recipe, she set out to experiment and came up with this unusual pie. Green peppercorns have a clean, fresh, mild taste and are found bottled or in cans.

Pepper Apple Pie

2 cups all-purpose flour
½ teaspoon salt
¾ cup vegetable shortening
5 tablespoons cold water
1 tablespoon white vinegar
2 tablespoons butter
1 heaping teaspoon crushed green
   peppercorns

4 to 5 tart apples, depending on
   size, peeled, cored and thinly
   sliced
½ cup sugar, additional for
   sprinkling
1 tablespoon lemon juice

In a bowl, sift together the flour and salt, cut in the shortening until it resembles coarse crumbs, and gradually add the cold water and vinegar until a soft dough forms. Divide the dough evenly into two balls and refrigerate until needed.

Preheat oven to 450 degrees.

In a small saucepan, melt butter and add the crushed peppercorns. Place the apples, butter mixture and sugar in a large bowl, and toss until well mixed. Sprinkle with lemon juice.

Roll out one of the balls of dough, and place it in a 10-inch pie plate. Spread the apple mixture over the dough. Roll out the other dough ball, place it on top of the apples, and crimp the edges to seal. Pierce dough with a fork in several places to allow steam to vent during cooking. Sprinkle a little additional sugar on top and bake for 10 minutes. Reduce heat to 350 degrees and bake an additional 40 minutes, or until the crust is lightly golden.

Makes six servings

Market Customer: Cheryl Elliott

Rose geranium leaves are available in the spring. This cake was made by Cheryl Elliott for sampling at one of the Market's herb festivals. It may seem that the geraniums don't do much, since they are discarded early in the recipe, but they do impart a distinct flavor to the butter and, ultimately, the cake.

Rose Geranium Pound Cake

12 rose geranium leaves
½ pound (2 sticks) butter
1 cup sugar
3 eggs, separated

1¾ cups all-purpose flour
½ cup half and half
1 teaspoon vanilla extract

Firmly press six of the geranium leaves around each stick of butter. Wrap in plastic wrap and refrigerate overnight. The next morning, unwrap butter, and remove and discard geranium leaves. Let the butter soften at room temperature for 30 minutes. Bring eggs to room temperature at the same time.

Preheat oven to 300 degrees.

Grease an 8- or 9-inch tube pan.

In a large mixing bowl, cream the butter, gradually adding ½ cup of the sugar. Beat until light and fluffy. Add egg yolks one at a time, beating well after each addition. Alternately add the flour and half and half. Stir in vanilla.

With the egg whites at room temperature, beat them until soft peaks form. Add remaining ½ cup of sugar, 1 tablespoon at a time, beating until stiff peaks form. Stir about 1 cup of this mixture into butter. Gently fold in the remaining egg-white mixture. Pour batter into prepared pan. Bake for 45 to 60 minutes, or until a cake tester comes out clean. Cool in pan for 15 minutes, remove, and cool completely before serving.

Makes eight servings

Market Customer: Jeanne Shutt

Jeanne Shutt, although not a native Philadelphian, frequently visits the city since moving to nearby Wayne many years ago. She hosts many a party on the Main Line for friends and family members. Jeanne loves to cook, and especially to bake. Being in the hospitality business as a vice president of sales and marketing, she often has the opportunity to entertain and recommend attractions to clients. Reading Terminal Market is her favorite Philadelphia destination—it appeals to everyone who enjoys food, beverages, eclectic shopping and people-watching. This recipe is perfect for any occasion. Jeanne loves to serve it for Fourth of July celebrations, with its colorful use of strawberries and blueberries. Many of the ingredients are available at the Market.

Shutt Strawberry and Blueberry Yogurt Bundt Cake

2½ cups all-purpose flour

½ teaspoon baking soda

½ teaspoon salt

Grated zest of 1 lemon (Meyer lemons preferable), reserve 1 tablespoon juice

½ pound (2 sticks) butter, room temperature

2 cups sugar

3 eggs

1 teaspoon Mexican vanilla extract

8 ounces plain or vanilla Greek yogurt

6 ounces fresh strawberries, diced

6 ounces fresh blueberries

4 ounces of granola

GLAZE

1¼ cups powdered sugar

1 to 2 tablespoons lemon juice

½ cup chopped pecans for topping

Preheat oven to 325 degrees.

Grease and flour a 10-inch Bundt pan and set aside.

In a bowl, stir together flour, baking soda and salt. Mix in the lemon zest, and set aside.

With an electric mixer, cream together the butter and sugar until light and fluffy. Beat in eggs one at a time, and stir in the reserved tablespoon of lemon juice and vanilla. Alternately beat in flour mixture and yogurt, mixing just until incorporated. Gently stir in strawberries, blueberries and granola. Pour batter into Bundt pan. Bake 60 to 65 minutes, or until a wooden toothpick inserted into center of the cake comes out clean.

Allow to cool 25 minutes in the pan, turn out onto a wire rack, and cool completely.

When cake is cooled, make glaze. In a small bowl, whisk together powdered sugar and lemon juice. Drizzle glaze over top of cake, letting it drip down the sides. Sprinkle with chopped pecans.

Makes 12 to 16 slices

Noodle Pudding

Janie Auspitz of the Famous 4th Street Cookie Company would not give out any cookie recipes. But she was more than happy to give a recipe for noodle pudding, taken from her mother's handwritten collection. Janie remembers her working in the kitchen, making different desserts and trying them out on her. Her mother went to the "a little this, a little that" school of cooking. It's now been standardized so you too can enjoy.

6 ounces capellini pasta	2½ tablespoons sugar
¼ pound (1 stick) butter	3 eggs, beaten
4 ounces cream cheese, softened	2 cups milk
and broken into pieces	Cinnamon and sugar for sprinkling

Preheat oven to 350 degrees.

Grease an 8-inch square baking pan.

In a large saucepan, cook noodles in lightly salted water until al dente. Drain, but do not rinse. Place noodles in a bowl. Melt the butter in a small saucepan. Pour half the melted butter into the drained noodles along with the cream cheese, and mix to combine. Sprinkle in the sugar, and mix again.

Place the noodles in the prepared baking pan and add the remaining melted butter. Beat the eggs with the milk, pour over the noodle mixture, sprinkle with cinnamon and sugar, and bake for about 45 minutes to 1 hour, or until cooked through and custard is set.

Makes four servings

Pumpkin Walnut Muffins

These delicious muffins from Metropolitan Bakery can be prepared using pumpkin puree from seasonal fresh sugar pumpkins or enjoyed year round using canned pumpkin. Sugar or pie pumpkins are small with firm, sweet flesh and are excellent for cooking. The large "jack-o-lantern" pumpkins tend to have a stringy, watery interior. Whether you use the sugar pumpkin or canned pumpkin puree, these muffins will be gobbled up for sure.

2 cups all-purpose flour
1½ teaspoons ground cinnamon
1⅛ teaspoons baking powder
1⅛ teaspoons baking soda
½ teaspoon salt
¼ teaspoon ground ginger
¼ teaspoon ground nutmeg
⅛ teaspoon ground cloves
1 cup granulated sugar
1 cup firmly packed dark brown sugar

5 tablespoons cold, unsalted butter, cut into small cubes
3 large eggs
1 cup, plus 2 tablespoons pumpkin puree, canned or fresh (see Pumpkin puree, page 19)
⅓ cup milk
1 teaspoon pure vanilla extract
1⅓ cups chopped walnuts, toasted (see How to toast nuts, page 19)

Preheat oven to 375 degrees.

Butter 12 standard (2½-inch) muffin cups.

In the bowl of a stand-up mixer, sift together flour, cinnamon, baking powder, baking soda, salt, ginger, nutmeg and cloves. Stir in granulated and brown sugars. Add butter and toss. With a paddle attachment at low speed, mix butter into flour mixture until the mixture resembles coarse meal.

In a medium bowl, whisk eggs and stir into the flour mixture. Stir in pumpkin puree, milk and vanilla until just blended. With a rubber spatula, fold in walnuts.

Spoon batter evenly into prepared muffin pan cups. Bake 15 to 20 minutes, or until a toothpick inserted in center of muffin comes out clean. Cool the muffins in the pan 5 minutes. Remove from pan and cool completely on wire racks.

Makes 12 muffins

Pumpkin puree: Preheat oven to 375 degrees. Cut one sugar pumpkin in half and scoop out seeds. Place pumpkin halves, cut side down, in a roasting pan. Add 1 cup water to pan and bake 45 minutes, or until skin wrinkles. Remove pumpkin from pan. When cool enough to handle, scoop out flesh. Press flesh through a fine sieve set over a bowl. Discard contents in sieve, then line it with a double layer of cheesecloth and set over another bowl. Spoon the puree into the sieve and allow it to drain overnight in the refrigerator.

How to toast nuts: Toasting nuts releases their natural oils. If toasted too long, nuts become bitter, so it's best to toast lightly to bring out a robust, nutty flavor. Preheat oven to 325 degrees. Spread nuts evenly on a baking sheet. Bake on the center oven rack for 10 to 12 minutes, or until fragrant and toasted. Cool.

The Metropolitan Bakery.

Termini's Chocolate Mousse with Rum

This mousse is a favorite of the Termini family. It was shared with us by Barbara Termini, Vincent's wife, from Termini Brothers Bakery.

8 ounces semisweet chocolate
2 tablespoons butter, at room
   temperature

4 eggs, separated
¼ cup light or dark rum
1 cup heavy cream

Melt the chocolate in the top of a double boiler over barely simmering water. Whisk in the butter, then the egg yolks, one at a time. Whisk in the rum. Remove from heat. If the mousse binds up, add more rum until it becomes smooth.

In a separate bowl, whip the egg whites with a balloon whisk or piano-wire whisk until they hold a soft shape. Stir a third of the beaten egg whites into the mousse, then fold in the remaining whites. In the same bowl, whip the cream to a soft peak, and fold it into the mousse. Refrigerate for several hours before serving.

Makes eight servings

A section of the Termini Brothers display.

Beverage
Merchants

BLUE MOUNTAIN VINEYARDS has been producing first-class "Old World" wines in the heart of the Lehigh Valley (an American Viticulture Area) for over 25 years. Known for earthy, complex reds and crisp, clean whites, Blue Mountain, owned by winemaker Joseph Greff, is proud to be a Market mainstay for the last 11 years. With nearly 100 national and international awards already, they have a wine for every palette. Blue Mountain prides itself on the knowledge of its staff and its excellent customer service. Whether you are a wine novice or the virtual second coming of Bacchus himself, they can help you find the perfect bottle for any meal or occasion. Blue Mountain also offers private tasting parties, custom labels and an assortment of wine accessories.

Four Seasons Juice Bar, owned by Brian Wang, will refresh the weary shopper or tired tourist with a healthy, tasty beverage of freshly blended fruit and/or vegetables. In a Market noted for the freshest farm-to-city produce, it's a natural to have a stand offering drinks made with a great mix of all-natural ingredients. All drinks are made without sugar, preservatives or additives. The Four Seasons counter displays a cornucopia of apples, bananas, carrots, cucumbers, celery, ginger, kiwis and—for the adventurous—wheatgrass. Their experienced staff is more than willing to help you make selections. Any or all combinations can be blended to produce drinks and smoothies in an assortment of very interesting colors.

Old City Coffee was founded in 1984 and is owned by Ruth and Isaac Treatman. Its original location is in the Old City section of Philadelphia; the store is still there. In 1988, the Treatmans opened a second store at the Reading Terminal Market where it became an immediate success. It is a 100 percent Philadelphia metro-operated business with a dedicated, knowledgeable staff to help you choose varieties, roasts and brewing techniques. They roast only the best grade of arabica high-grown coffee. By avoiding commercial roasters and wholesalers, Old City can serve customers great coffee at a reasonable price. Roasted in tiny batches, their coffee is guaranteed to be the freshest available. Old City Coffee has been recognized by *Philadelphia* magazine and *City Paper* for "Best Coffee Beans," and they placed first in Zagat's survey for "Best Bang for the Buck." The company has also been noted in *The New Yorker* and in *Espresso from Bean to Cup* by Nick Jurich. Stop by and enjoy a cup of freshly brewed coffee, espresso, cappuccino or their specialty caffe latte, along with a delicious baked good as a perfect accompaniment.

Tea Leaf is a small, elegant shop owned by Lynnette Chen. It is the only place in the Market devoted entirely to tea and tea accessories. Lynnette's love of tea and her desire to give consumers an alternative to coffee made her open this shop, and she has enjoyed success since 1995. This cozy spot is frequented by many regular customers and by tea lovers from around the world. Lynnette, who is friendly and very knowledgeable, will guide you in making the perfect cup of tea. Tea Leaf offers an incredible range of loose teas from Europe and Asia, including black and oolong teas, flavored teas, green teas, white teas, as well as decaffeinated and herbal teas. Some of the more exotic varieties include Moroccan Mint, White Mutan, Dragon Phoenix Pearl, Chocolate Black Tea and Bourbon Vanilla.

Fruit and Vegetable Smoothies

If you start craving a refreshing smoothie or juice drink while at the Market, head over to Four Seasons Juice Bar. They use only fresh fruit and vegetables—and wheatgrass, if requested. Here are two healthy fruit smoothie recipes and a vegetable-and-fruit smoothie you can whip up in minutes. No added sugar is necessary. The sweetness comes from the fruit, honey and/or yogurt. Other combinations of fruit and vegetables may be used. So be creative!

Mixed Berry Smoothie

2 cups mixed fruits (blackberries, strawberries, raspberries)
1 cup milk

In a blender or food processor, combine all ingredients and blend until smooth.

Makes two servings

Strawberry and Banana Smoothie

2 bananas
1½ cups strawberries
½ cup Greek vanilla yogurt

½ cup milk
2 teaspoons honey

In a blender or food processor, combine all ingredients and blend until smooth.

Makes two servings

Green Smoothie

1 cup baby spinach, firmly packed

1 cup chopped cucumbers, seedless and peeled

1 banana, sliced

1¼ cups chopped apple (1 large), unpeeled

½ cup chopped canned pineapple, drained, reserve 3 tablespoons juice

Water

In a food processor or blender, combine spinach, cucumbers, banana, apple and pineapple, and reserved pineapple juice. Blend until smooth, adding enough water to reach desired consistency.

Makes two servings

A selection of ingredients for smoothies.

Lynnette's Perfect Cup of Tea

Lynnette Chen uses one basic method of brewing tea, regardless of the variety. Black tea, such as Darjeeling and Lapsang souchong, is made from tea leaves that are fermented, while flavored black tea is made from black tea blended with fruits, nuts, spices and/or herbs. Oolong is a common blend and is a combination of green and black teas. Green teas, such as Cherry Blossom, Pomegranate Green and Japanese Genmaicha, are made from leaves that have been steamed. White teas, including White Earl Grey and White Mutan, are made from tea leaves that have been simply picked and dried without undergoing a heat treatment. Herbal teas are a blend of flowers, leaves, roots, seeds, fruits and/or nuts, and are often brewed as health remedies. Lynnette's selection of herbal teas includes organic ginger root, hibiscus, detox blend and spearmint. The decaffeinated teas at Tea Leaf are made using a high-pressure process without solvents of any kind and include Ceylon, Darjeeling and Sencha.

TO MAKE A GOOD CUP OF TEA:

Preheat the teapot by pouring boiling water into it, and let sit for about 5 minutes. Discard water and add tea. Use 1 teaspoon of tea leaves per cup of water. Pour boiling water over the leaves, and steep the tea. Green tea should steep for 3 minutes, black and herbal teas for 5. Serve, relax and enjoy.

Mochaccino

Mochaccino is a great pick-me-up from Old City Coffee. To prepare this properly, you need a cappuccino maker equipped with a steam wand, which has become a staple in a lot of homes. The sweetness is adjustable. To get the foam, start with very cold milk and a pitcher that has been in the freezer for several minutes. Steam and allow to rest a few minutes to help stiffen the foam. Old City Coffee makes this recipe with its 6-Bean Espresso blend of freshly roasted and ground arabica beans, and brews it with a thick layer of *crema,* which describes the top layer of foam.

12 ounces whole milk
1 heaping tablespoon Dutch cocoa
Sugar to taste
4 ounces brewed espresso coffee

Whipped cream flavored with
    French vanilla syrup, optional
Semisweet chocolate shavings

Steam milk in a steamer pot and set aside.

In a mug, combine cocoa and sugar. Add espresso and whisk quickly to dissolve cocoa. Pour the hot milk into the mug, and follow with the milk foam. Top with whipped cream, and garnish with chocolate shavings, if desired.

Makes one serving

Old City Coffee Chocolate Sauce

The following chocolate sauce from Old City Coffee is made using their popular 6-Bean Espresso. The sauce is perfect for latte art, dessert plate decoration, topping on ice cream or a perfect, all-natural glass of chocolate milk. The recipe can be halved to make one cup of chocolate sauce.

1 shot (1½ ounces) Old City Coffee
6-Bean Espresso
Water
1½ cups granulated sugar

1 cup unsweetened cocoa powder
½ teaspoon salt
1 teaspoon pure vanilla extract

Pour the espresso into the bottom of a one-cup measuring cup. Fill with water to reach one-cup capacity. Pour mixture into a saucepan.

Add sugar and cocoa powder to saucepan and heat over medium low heat until dissolved. Turn off heat, remove from burner and stir in salt and vanilla.

Allow mixture to cool. Keep any unused sauce in refrigerator.

Makes about two cups

A cup of java and a slice of cake at Old City Coffee.

Sangria

While Blue Mountain Vineyards' wines are perfect "table wines," they can be used for something a little more fun. Here is Blue Mountain Vineyards' recipe for a dynamite sangria that is sure to be the hit of your next party. The recipe can be doubled or tripled.

1 750-milliliter bottle of Blue
    Mountain Vineyards cabernet
    sauvignon or shiraz
1 pint fresh strawberries, cleaned,
    hulled and cut in half
1 large orange, cut in slices
1 lime cut in slices

10 to 12 maraschino cherries and a
    splash of cherry juice
1 20-ounce can chunk pineapple
    with juice or 1 6-ounce can
    pineapple juice
¼ cup brandy

Mix ingredients together in a large pitcher and chill overnight.

Serve over ice and enjoy!

Tips: If more sweetness is desired, add cane sugar a teaspoon at a time to taste, or use Blue Mountain Vineyards' semisweet Victoria's Passion instead of the drier wines. Also, feel free to use as much fruit as you want; eating the wine-soaked fruit is the best part!

Makes six servings

Dairy and Cheese Merchants

ICE CREAM WAS not invented in Philadelphia, but Philadelphia is considered by many to be the ice cream capital of the world. So what do most out-of-towners want to sample when they visit Philadelphia, and what do Philadelphians need to fulfill a craving for a sweet? The answer is a scoop of hand-dipped ice cream from Bassetts, the oldest ice cream brand in the nation. "Not only have generations of families enjoyed ice cream at the Market, but they have also taken many a pint home," says Michael Strange, the current owner and great-great-grandson of the founder. Bassetts began in 1861, when Lewis Dubois Bassett, a Quaker schoolteacher, began making ice cream in the back yard of his farm in Salem, New Jersey, in a churn that was turned by a mule. He sold his ice cream, along with homegrown produce, from a stand on Market Street in Philadelphia. In 1892, along with many other merchants, Bassett moved to the newly built Reading Terminal Market. Lewis Lafayette Bassett Jr. perfected the recipe handed down from his grandfather, and would comb the fruit and spice stands to find ingredients for exotic, new flavors, such as guava, kiwi, papaya, yellow tomato, and even borsht sherbet, specially prepared for a visit by Soviet premier Nikita Khruschchev. Over the years, the reins and secret recipes were handed down, once to Ann Bassett, the great-granddaughter, and then to Michael Strange. Bassetts, like other original Reading Terminal Market "families," has survived the

Roger Bassett and Michael Strange at Bassetts Ice Cream counter.

Civil War and the Great Depression. It has thrived through six generations and is the oldest and the only original family-run establishment operating in the Market.

Another Market tradition is Downtown Cheese, owned by Jack Morgan. He got his start in the cheese business over 40 years ago at the famed Ashbourne Market in Elkins Park. Jack is passionate about his cheeses. There are over 150 different cheeses at any given time on display in his shop. They range from traditional cheeses like Brie, which is still one of their most popular, to aged Gouda and Gruyère to a mild sheep's milk cheese from the French Basque region called Istava, and a cow's milk medium strong triple crème blue cheese, St. Agur. In addition to cheeses, Jack offers some specialty meats including French hams, Spanish Jamon Serrano, and an incredibly expensive, hard-to-find ham from the black hoof pig, Jamon Iberico de Bellota.

Salumeria, a long-established cheese shop, Italian deli and grocery, conveys the essence of the Market. Ed Sciamanna, the owner, has captured the Italian flavor of his offerings with an abundance of domestic and international cheeses and displays of prosciutti, salami, as well as imported cured Italian meats. In one corner, large earthenware jars are filled with Gaeta, Kalamata and other varieties of olives. Both familiar and hard-to-find items are in stock, from domestic mortadella and pancetta to buffalo milk and truffle butter, butter of Parma, black truffle slices and paste, roasted red peppers with pine nuts and raisins and Mostarda, a fruit jam infused with a mustard essence. At the takeout counter, customers wait patiently for their favorite specialty sandwich or salad. One popular hoagie is a unique version made with marinated artichoke hearts and a special house vinaigrette that many customers call phenomenal. At Salumeria, you may have come just to buy cheese, but you will leave with so much more.

A new and very welcome addition to the Market is the Valley Shepherd Creamery, owned by former real estate developer and engineer Eran Wajswol. He has a small sheep and goat farm located in Long Valley, New Jersey. Some 700 sheep, goats and cows provide milk from the farm. At the store in the Market, cheeses are made daily (in full view of the customers) and over 25 varieties are sold. The selections include a Cheddar-style cheese called Reading or Not, a strong blue cheese called Blue Me Away, a farmer's cheese called Phresh, and a Mozzarella called MozzaRTM. In addition to cheeses there are yogurts, and at Meltkraft, part of Valley Shepherd Creamery, they make specialty grilled cheese sandwiches. After barely six months of business, they have won the Best of Philly "grilled cheese." Valley Shepherd Creamery is a Market destination certain to satisfy your cheese cravings.

Ann Hazan's Pasta alla Norma

Although my family is from the Greek island of Chios and I love Greek food, my second favorite cuisine is Italian. This dish is from Catania, a city in Sicily. My brother, Nick, first told me about this sauce after reading about it in a mystery series. There are many stories of how this dish got its name. I believe the one that claims it was named in honor of the famous Italian opera, *Norma*. Regardless, the combination of eggplant, tomato sauce, ricotta salata and basil is exquisite. Ricotta salata, available at Market cheese shops, is made from goat's or sheep's milk pressed and salted (salata) to form a semi-firm cheese that can be crumbled or grated. It might be fun to experiment with other cheeses as well.

2 medium eggplants, peeled, and
  sliced into ½-inch-thick slices
Salt for eggplant
Canola oil and olive oil for frying
  eggplant
3 tablespoons extra virgin olive oil
4 garlic cloves, minced
1 28-ounce can Italian plum
  tomatoes, drained and chopped

Pinch of dried oregano
Freshly ground pepper to taste
1 pound spaghetti
8 to 10 fresh basil leaves (some for
  garnish)
6 ounces ricotta salata cheese

Place eggplant slices on paper towels, sprinkle salt on both sides, and let sit for 15 to 20 minutes. Rinse slices and gently squeeze out excess water. Place on clean paper towels and pat dry.

In a large skillet, heat a combination of canola and olive oil (about ⅛-inch deep) on medium-high heat. When hot, slip in eggplant slices and fry until golden on both sides. (If you need to cook eggplant in batches, add more oil as needed.) Remove from pan, allowing excess oil to drip off, then plate and set aside. Reserve 8 small eggplant slices for topping each serving. When cool enough to handle, cut remaining slices into 1-inch cubes and reserve.

In another skillet, heat extra virgin olive oil. Add garlic and cook 1 minute. Add tomatoes, oregano and pepper, and cook 15 to 20 minutes. Add reserved eggplant cubes and simmer 5 to 10 minutes longer.

While sauce is cooking, cook pasta. Bring a large pot of water to a boil, add pasta, bring to a second boil, stir, turn heat off, cover pot and allow pasta to sit in hot water for approximately 9 minutes. Check pasta to see if it is done. If not, put cover back on for another minute or so. Drain pasta, reserving about ⅓ cup of pasta water. Add some of the reserved pasta water to sauce to thin it to desired consistency.

Place a mound of pasta on each plate, and distribute reserved eggplant slices over each serving. Chop half of the basil leaves and add on top of eggplant. Top with grated ricotta salata, and garnish with whole basil leaves. Serve.

Makes four servings

Caprese Salad

One of the wonderful things about shopping at the Reading Terminal Market is the willingness of the merchants and their staff not only to assist you, but also to give you some great ideas for preparing or using their food items. Salumeria carries a wide and interesting variety of cheeses. One of their knowledgeable staff members, Micah Chamberlain, shared a recipe using their own buffalo mozzarella. This first-course dish is as delightful to the eye as it is to the palate.

2 heirloom tomatoes (other varieties of ripe tomatoes may be used)
½-pound ball buffalo mozzarella
1 large peach, pitted
¼ cup chopped fresh basil (reserve a few whole basil leaves for garnish)

Salt and pepper to taste
Extra virgin olive oil for drizzling
Balsamic vinegar (optional)

Note: Thinly slice tomatoes, mozzarella and peach.

Place alternating layers of tomatoes, mozzarella and peach on four salad plates or a platter. Top with chopped basil, and season with salt and pepper to taste. Sprinkle with olive oil and a little balsamic vinegar, if desired. Garnish with whole basil leaves. Serve.

Makes four servings

Cheese Appetizer with Mostarda

The next time you stop at Salumeria for cheese, be sure to check out some of their other great items like Mostarda, a fruit jam infused with a mustard essence. It pairs perfectly with Salumeria's many cheeses. Varieties include pear, plum, crab apple and green apple. Here is a suggestion for a tasty appetizer for all occasions that only takes a few minutes to put together.

Using crostini or any kind of cracker, spread or top with cheese. Suggested varieties include triple crème brie, any type of sheep's milk cheese, fresh chèvre, fresh mozzarella or manchego. Add a small dollop of Mostarda and serve.

The cheese display at Salumeria.

Cheese Fondue

This fantastic fondue is from Jack Morgan, the owner of Downtown Cheese. He carries an extensive variety of cheeses and specialty meats. Jack's shop specializes in handmade artisan cheeses from all over the globe. Fondue may be served with toasted buttered bread (for the grilled cheese effect), blanched vegetables, seared meat, hardboiled quail eggs, apples, pears or your favorite food for dipping.

1 tablespoon butter	3 to 4 whole black peppercorns
1 shallot, sliced	½ cup heavy cream
¾ cup white wine	1 cup shredded Gruyère
¼ cup sherry wine	½ cup shredded Appenzeller
½ teaspoon Dijon mustard	½ cup shredded Emmentaler
1 bay leaf	Pinch of nutmeg

In a shallow saucepan, melt butter and cook shallots until translucent. Add wine, sherry, Dijon mustard, bay leaf and peppercorns, and cook over medium heat until reduced to about ¾ of a cup. Strain and keep the liquid. Discard the peppercorns and bay leaf.

Put the liquid back into the pan, add cream and simmer for 5 minutes. While still at a simmer, add all the cheeses gradually, whisking continuously. When blended and smooth, add nutmeg and pour into a fondue pot. Start dipping!

Makes four servings

Cheese Sauces for Pasta

These two pasta sauces can be prepared within 30 minutes. All the cheeses used are available at the Market's cheese shops. In fact, all the ingredients can be found at the Market. You can use your favorite pasta shape, but when making cream sauces, fresh cut pasta is recommended because it absorbs the sauce more readily than dried. Parmigiano-Reggiano is an aged, artisan cheese. It is made in northern Italy, in Reggio Emilia, Parma, Modena, and certain parts of Bologna and Mantua. Locatelli is the brand name for a high-quality Romano cheese. According to some of the cheese merchants at the Market, customers are very specific about which of these cheeses they prefer to use.

Alfredo Sauce

1 cup heavy cream
3 tablespoons unsalted butter
⅔ cup freshly grated Parmigiano-Reggiano or Locatelli Romano cheese

Freshly ground pepper to taste
Freshly grated nutmeg to taste
Cayenne pepper to taste

In a heavy saucepan, combine heavy cream and butter. Simmer for approximately 15 minutes, or until sauce is slightly reduced and thickened. Add cheese, pepper, nutmeg and cayenne, and stir over low heat 1 to 2 minutes longer. Toss with pasta.

Makes enough sauce for one pound of pasta

Gorgonzola Cream Sauce

¾ cup dry vermouth

1 cup heavy cream

¼ pound sweet Gorgonzola cheese, crumbled

2 to 4 tablespoons freshly grated Parmigiano-Reggiano or Locatelli Romano cheese

Freshly ground pepper to taste

Freshly grated nutmeg to taste

In a heavy saucepan, bring vermouth to a boil and reduce by about half. Add heavy cream and simmer uncovered about 10 to 15 minutes, or until slightly thickened. Stir in both cheeses. Add pepper and nutmeg. Simmer over very low heat, stirring constantly until smooth and creamy, approximately 2 minutes. Toss with pasta.

Makes enough sauce for one pound of pasta

A selection of cheeses from the Market.

Goat Cheese Soufflé

This soufflé is baked in a shallow, oval baking dish instead of in a traditional soufflé bowl. The combination of goat, Gruyère and cheddar cheeses (available at all Market cheese shops) is a sure palate pleaser, and this recipe will soon become a regular menu item for breakfast, brunch, lunch or a light evening supper.

1⅓ cups light cream	4 ounces goat cheese, crumbled
1⅓ cups milk	3 ounces Gruyère cheese, grated
½ carrot, sliced	2 ounces cheddar or Parmesan
1 small onion, quartered	cheese, grated
Sprig of fresh thyme	Pinch of salt
3 ounces butter	Freshly ground black pepper to taste
1½ tablespoons all-purpose flour	Pinch of cayenne pepper
5 eggs, separated	Pinch of nutmeg

Preheat oven to 450 degrees.

Brush a 12-inch oval baking dish with melted butter.

Place cream and milk into a saucepan. Add carrot, onion and thyme. Slowly bring to a boil, take off heat and let sit for about 10 minutes. Strain and discard vegetables.

In a saucepan, melt butter, add flour and cook for 1 to 2 minutes. Gradually whisk in the strained cream and milk. Bring to a full boil, then lower heat. Continue whisking until mixture thickens. Cool slightly.

Add the egg yolks, goat cheese, Gruyère and most of the cheddar or Parmesan (leave some for topping). Season with salt, black pepper, cayenne and nutmeg.

Whisk egg whites until stiff and fold them gently, using a flat spatula, into the cheese mixture. Pour into prepared dish and sprinkle with remaining cheese.

Place in oven and cook for 12 to 15 minutes, or until the sides and top are nicely puffed up and golden. The center should still be slightly creamy. Serve at once.

Makes six servings

Gougeres (Cheese Puffs)

Both authors make these savory hors d'oeuvres for gatherings of family and friends. For this recipe, nutmeg or curry powder can be substituted for the cayenne and paprika. Also minced fresh dill or chives may be added (after the eggs in the recipe). The cheeses used are available from your favorite fromager at the Market.

4 tablespoons (½ stick) unsalted
    butter
1 cup milk
¼ teaspoon salt
Dash of cayenne pepper
1 cup all-purpose flour
3 large eggs

½ teaspoon paprika
1 teaspoon chopped dill or chives,
    optional
½ cup grated Parmesan cheese
1½ cups Gruyère or Swiss cheese
Coarse salt for sprinkling

In a saucepan, bring butter, milk, salt and cayenne to a boil. Remove from heat and add flour all at once. Mix vigorously with a wooden spoon until mixture forms into a ball. Return pan to stove and cook over medium heat, stirring occasionally for 1 minute to remove excess moisture. Remove from heat and let cool slightly. Transfer to the bowl of a food processor. Add eggs, one at a time, and paprika. Blend for 10 to 15 seconds, or until well combined. Transfer the mixture to a mixing bowl and cool 10 minutes.

Preheat oven to 375 degrees.

Line a cookie sheet with parchment.

Reserve 1 tablespoon of the Parmesan cheese, add remainder of Parmesan and the Gruyère or Swiss cheese to the mixture. Stir just enough to incorporate. Using a tablespoon, drop a level spoonful of dough onto the lined baking sheet, spacing the gougeres about 2 inches apart. Sprinkle a few grains of coarse salt and a little of the reserved Parmesan cheese on each gougere. Bake about 30 minutes, or until nicely browned and crisp.

Makes about 30 gougeres

Ice Cream Slider

The Ice Cream Slider made its debut at the 2013 Reading Terminal Market Sidewalk Sizzle and Ice Cream Freeze festival. Lots of grilled foods and cold desserts were featured. Three days before the event, Michael Strange, the owner of Bassetts Ice Cream, and his nephew, Alex Bassett, were having dinner and thinking of an interesting way to serve their ice cream. Alex came up with this fun idea. Based on the popular hamburger sliders, why not have an ice cream version? They conspired with Glen Mueller Jr. of Mueller's Chocolate and Beiler's Donuts, and here it is.

¾ cup white chocolate chips
4 glazed donuts
4 large scoops of chocolate ice cream, softened and molded into 4 patties, then refrozen

Raspberry sauce for topping
Caramel sauce for topping

In a heavy saucepan or in a microwave, melt white chocolate chips. Spread thinly on a parchment-lined cookie sheet. Cool to set and cut into four 3-inch squares (looks just like a piece of cheese).

Split each glazed donut horizontally. Place the frozen ice cream patties on top of one half of each donut. Top with white chocolate squares. Put raspberry sauce in one squeeze bottle and caramel sauce in another. Top with either sauce. Place other half of donuts on top. Serve immediately.

Makes four sliders

Marinated Vegetables

Although many customers frequent Salumeria for their fine selection of cheeses, they also do a bustling business with their Italian groceries and deli stand. This recipe is one of Ed Sciamanna's favorites. It's easy to make, and varying the vegetables seasonally will always keep it interesting. This is a colorful addition to any buffet table.

DRESSING
½ cup chopped flat-leaf parsley
1 cup extra virgin olive oil
¼ cup lemon juice
1 teaspoon salt
1 teaspoon pepper
3 medium garlic cloves, minced

VEGETABLES
1 small zucchini, cut lengthwise and sliced into ¼-inch-thick pieces
1 yellow squash, cut lengthwise and sliced into ¼-inch pieces
¼ pound mushrooms, cleaned and sliced
1 red bell pepper, cut into strips
1 head Bibb lettuce

To make the dressing, combine the parsley, olive oil, lemon juice, salt, pepper and garlic in a blender or food processor, or shake in a jar. Set aside.

Place the zucchini, yellow squash, mushrooms and red pepper in a bowl and toss them with the dressing. Allow to marinate 1 to 2 hours. Place the lettuce leaves on a platter or in a bowl. Using a slotted spoon, place the vegetables on top of the lettuce, and sprinkle with the reserved dressing.

Makes four servings

Mrs. B's Apple Crisp

Grandmother's apple crisp is one of the Bassett family's favorite desserts. It is served with what has always been—and still is—their most popular flavor: vanilla. Bassetts Ice Cream has won numerous awards, including Best of Philly for several years, and it has been featured on the Travel Channel's *All-Time Ice Cream Paradise.*

Butter for greasing pan	1 teaspoon ground cinnamon
5 large, tart apples (such as Granny Smith or Rome), peeled, cored and sliced	¾ cup all-purpose flour
	3 tablespoons butter
	1 cup brown sugar
½ cup water	Vanilla ice cream

Preheat oven to 350 degrees.

Butter a 9-inch square baking pan.

Place apple slices in prepared pan. In a bowl, combine the water and cinnamon and pour over the apples. Place the flour in another bowl, and add the butter and brown sugar. Work the mixture into coarse crumbs and sprinkle the crumb mixture over the apples.

Bake for approximately 1 hour, until lightly golden. Serve warm or at room temperature with ice cream.

Makes six servings

The Sweet Sheep Grilled Cheese

Valley Shepherd Creamery strives to create artisan, award-winning, cave-aged cheeses and dairy products. At their Reading Terminal Market location, they are well known for making and selling cheeses (cow's, sheep's and goat's milk varieties). At Meltkraft, a part of Valley Shepherd Creamery, they work to create original and unusual grilled cheese sandwiches, and were awarded Best of Philly. Also available is their homemade ketchup along with an assortment of sides. This outstanding grilled cheese is made with a spiced speculoos cookie butter spread. Traditionally, this Belgian spread is made with speculoos cookies or "Biscoff" cookies. The chef at Meltkraft has shared her quick version using ginger snaps, which produces an equally good product.

2 cups Valley Shepherd whipped sheep milk ricotta

1 cup mascarpone cheese

10 slices soft brioche sandwich bread

¾ cup blackberry jam

1 cup hulled and diced strawberries

1 cup diced peaches

½ cup cleaned blackberries, cut into quarters

¾ cup miniature semisweet chocolate chips

1 cup speculoos cookie butter (see Note)

½ cup softened unsalted butter

Valley Shepherd Creamery and Meltkraft, specializing in local cheeses and dairy products.

In a bowl, mix together ricotta and mascarpone.

On a clean, dry surface, lay out five slices of the brioche. Spread equal parts black-berry jam on each slice. Place a large spoonful of the mascarpone ricotta mix on top of jam (it may be helpful to use a piping bag) until all the mixture is used.

Evenly divide strawberries, peaches, blackberries and chocolate chips among each slice. Spread the speculoos cookie butter on the remaining five slices of brioche and place on top of the first slices.

Spread the softened butter in a thin layer on the outer parts of the brioche. Grill in either a panini press or in a hot pan. Slice and serve hot.

Makes five servings

Note: If speculoos is too hard to find, here's how to make it. Place 2 cups of gin-ger snaps in the bowl of a food processor and blend to very fine crumbs. Add 4 tablespoons of softened unsalted butter, and process until a smooth paste forms (similar to consistency of peanut butter). Refrigerate leftover portion and bring to room temperature when using.

Meat and Poultry Merchants

SINCE 1892, READING Terminal Market has offered its customers a wonderful variety of quality meats and poultry.

The Border Springs Lamb Farm stall is now occupied by La Divisa Meats. Border Springs was America's first farm dedicated to lamb. They carried a wide assortment of cuts, from shanks and legs to racks, chops and ground lamb, seven different types of fresh sausages all in lamb casings and a rotating selection of charcuterie. In addition there were unique sandwiches such as pulled lamb shoulder, lamb burgers and smoked leg of lamb, together with prepared foods to have for lunch in the Market or to take home and heat for dinner. Their lamb tacos and lamb ribs became Market favorites. The farm's owner and shepherd, Craig Rogers, is a former professor of engineering at Virginia Tech and was dean of the College of Engineering at the University of South Carolina. It was at Virginia Tech, while a spectator at sheep dog trials (like in the movie *Babe*), that Craig became fascinated by these awesome working dogs. When the time was right, he purchased a "retirement" farm. Three days later, six sheep and a trained border collie were in residence. He then started competing nationally with his dogs. He now has a couple thousand sheep and several working dogs. "So much for retirement," says Craig. He's as busy as ever and loving it! "Border Springs" is a combination of Border collies and the farm's location in Patrick Springs, Virginia. Border Springs has sold lamb to famous chefs all along the East Coast and the South. Now La Divisa's Nick Macri makes his fine meats available to consumers in the Reading Terminal Market.

Giunta's Prime Shop's owner Rob Passio is upholding a strong tradition by following in the Giunta family's footsteps. The family migrated from their native Sicily in the early 1900s and settled in the Italian Market section of South Philadelphia. Charles Jr. was the fourth generation of the Giunta family to hone the family craft. He started in Reading Terminal Market in 1982, and he stayed until 1990. Sixteen years later and with 16 years more experience, Charles returned to the Market in 2006. The Giunta's display case is lined with a variety of natural and organic cuts of steak, dry-aged beef, freshly ground meat, local lamb, veal, homemade sausages and all-natural poultry products.

Martin's Quality Meats & Sausages has been in the Market since 1983, when it opened as Guinta's Prime Meats. In 1987, Martin Giunta took it over as a sausage store, along with a full line of meats and game, and the location then became Martin's Quality Meats & Sausages. As Martin Giunta's interest in sausage-making grew, he opened a sausage plant in South Philly, where he began producing many kinds of sausages, including hot and mild Italian, fresh apple sausage, luganega sausage with Romano cheese and parsley, chicken apple sausage and more. In addition to their considerable variety of sausages, the store carries several different cuts of veal and steak; freshly ground pork, lamb and beef; beef brisket; pigs feet and baby back ribs.

Hatville farmer Charles Godshall, the original owner of Godshall's Poultry, began selling his products at the Market in 1916. In 1935, his son, Ernie, took over the business. The current owners are Ernie's nephew, Dean, and Steve Frankenfield. Chicken had always been their best seller, but today, chicken and turkey sales at the stand run about the same. Godshall's also sells their own turkey sausage, turkey bacon, sage stuffing and turkey parts, like giblets and necks for turkey stock as well as legs and drumsticks. In addition, they feature turkey versions of traditional beef cuts like chops, cutlets, scallopini, stew cubes and London broil.

Past Merchants of the Market

We have included recipes from past merchants in this new edition. Four generations of the same family made Harry G. Ochs & Son one of the longest-running family-owned businesses in the Market. Harry Ochs started there in 1906. Harry

After 105 years of operation, Harry G. Ochs meats closed its shop in 2011.

Ochs III took over the reins from his father in 1947, and continued selling only the finest, farm-raised prime meats. Harry's gregarious personality made the stand a centerpiece of Reading Terminal Market. He used to relate story after story about the Market, while deftly demonstrating his technique of boning a leg of lamb. He even cut meat for Joe DiMaggio and Julia Child when they visited Philadelphia. Harry was a highly visible figure during the Market's trying months of renovation and for many years until his passing in 2009. His business continued in its location until 2011.

Christian Moyer started his company in 1856, going door-to-door in the city with a horse and wagon, selling pork products. He developed his own recipe for scrapple, which he sold at the Market for many years. The Moyer's opened in the Market in 1904. Eugene M. Moyer & Son was well known for award-winning hams. The store was a part of the Market family for many years until it was sold in 1997.

A.A. Halteman's Poultry opened in the Market in 1943. They started by selling only dressed chickens and eggs. In 1960, Sonny Halteman took over the family business and saw many changes over the years. For example, people started wanting lunchmeats and cut-up, oven-ready chickens, so those items were added as well. Sonny eventually closed the business in 2006.

Siegfried's & Son German Gourmet was in operation in the Market for many years. The store was well known for imported and domestic meats and sausages as well as other German specialties. Siegfried's left the Market in 2000.

Ann Hazan's Roast Leg of Lamb with Orzo

This Greek dish is prepared for a traditional Easter dinner using the spring lamb available at the Market during this season. Orzo, which looks like long-grain rice, is actually a pasta made from semolina. It is excellent served with a sprinkling of freshly grated cheese alongside roasted lamb or chicken.

1 leg lamb, 3½ to 4 pounds
2 large garlic cloves, peeled and
   sliced in half
1 medium onion, thinly sliced
2 tablespoons olive oil
2 tablespoons unsalted butter
1 tablespoon oregano
Salt and freshly ground pepper to
   taste

2 cups canned Italian plum
   tomatoes, drained and chopped
½ cup water
3½ cups chicken stock
1½ cups orzo
Freshly grated Locatelli Romano
   cheese

Preheat oven to 350 degrees.

Make four 1-inch cuts in the lamb, and insert the garlic slivers into the cuts. Place lamb in a roasting pan and spread the onion around the lamb.

In a small saucepan, heat the oil and butter together and pour over the lamb. Season with oregano, salt and pepper. Place in the oven and cook for 10 to 15 minutes. Add the tomatoes and water and continue cooking for approximately 1½ to 2 hours, basting frequently with pan juices. During cooking, add more water to pan juices if necessary. A meat thermometer inserted into the thickest part of the meat should register 140 degrees for rare and 160 degrees for medium. Remove lamb, cover loosely with foil and keep warm.

Add the chicken stock to the roasting pan, stir in the orzo, return to the oven and cook for approximately 30 to 40 minutes, or until the liquid is absorbed. Slice the lamb and serve with the orzo, topped with a sprinkling of the grated cheese.

Makes four servings

Braised Veal Shanks

Harry Ochs, owner of Harry G. Ochs & Son, once a popular meat purveyor in the Market, shared many cooking tips and recipes with customers. This was one of his favorites.

6 to 8 veal shanks, about 2 inches thick
Olive oil for coating veal and vegetables
2 garlic cloves, finely chopped
½ cup chopped Italian flat-leaf parsley
1 tablespoon chopped fresh rosemary, or ½ teaspoon dried

4 carrots, diced
1 large onion, chopped
2 medium potatoes, quartered
Salt and freshly ground pepper to taste
2 cups white wine

Preheat oven to 350 degrees.

Generously coat veal shanks with olive oil. In a Dutch oven, brown shanks on both sides over medium heat for about 5 minutes per side. Add garlic, parsley and rosemary and cook for 1 to 2 minutes. Coat carrots, onion and potatoes with a little more olive oil and add them to the shanks. Season with salt and pepper and cook 2 to 3 minutes. Add wine.

Bake, covered, for approximately 1½ hours, or until veal is very tender and almost falling off the bone. If the wine evaporates too quickly during cooking, add more as necessary until shanks are tender. Uncover and cook 15 to 20 minutes longer to reduce sauce and brown shanks lightly.

Makes six to eight servings

Cider Stew

Steve Frankenfield's wife, Julie, has prepared this great harvest-time dish for her family for years. It's based on a beef stew recipe she found and adapted for the dark turkey cubes that Godshall's sells. If you use leftover cooked dark turkey meat, skip the steps for browning. The stew can also be made in a crock-pot after the meat is browned.

3 tablespoons all-purpose flour	½ cup water
¼ teaspoon crushed thyme	2 tablespoons red wine vinegar
2 teaspoons salt	1 stalk celery, diced
¼ teaspoon pepper	4 carrots, quartered
2 pounds turkey stew cubes	3 potatoes, peeled and quartered
3 tablespoons oil	2 onions, chopped
2 cups apple cider or apple juice	1 apple, chopped

In a plastic bag, combine flour, thyme, salt and pepper. Add meat and toss to coat.

In a Dutch oven, brown the meat in hot oil. Stir in cider, water and vinegar, cook and stir until boiling. Reduce heat, cover and simmer until turkey is tender, about 1 to 1½ hours.

Add the celery, carrots, potatoes, onions and apples to the turkey. Cook until vegetables are tender, about 30 to 40 minutes.

Makes six to eight servings

Curried Turkey and Rice

Here is a recipe from A.A. Halteman that they shared with us for our original Market cookbook. This dish can also be made with ground chicken.

1½ pounds ground turkey
1 medium onion, sliced
1½ cups long-grain rice, uncooked
3 cups water
1 cube chicken bouillon
1 tablespoon curry powder
2 garlic cloves, minced

½ teaspoon ground ginger
¼ teaspoon ground cinnamon
2 tablespoons peanut butter
1 teaspoon honey
½ cup raisins
½ teaspoon salt

In a large skillet over medium heat, cook the turkey and onion until lightly browned, stirring occasionally. Drain any fat that may have accumulated.

Add remaining ingredients. Bring to a boil, reduce heat to simmer, cover and cook about 25 minutes, stirring occasionally, until the rice is tender and the liquid has been absorbed. If necessary, add small amounts of hot water.

Makes six servings

Garlic Glazed Lamb Ribs

This recipe was from Border Springs Lamb Farm, and calls for a cut of lamb that most butchers don't have. They were hoping that a variation of these ribs would become their "signature" dish in the Market. The best way to eat these ribs is with your fingers, and clean the bone dry.

4 to 6 pounds Border Springs Lamb ribs (short ribs sometimes called Denver ribs)
Water
1¼ cups balsamic vinegar, divided
¼ cup olive oil
Salt and pepper to taste
3 tablespoons chopped garlic
3 tablespoons chopped fresh rosemary
¼ cup honey

Place ribs in a pan, add enough water to cover and braise for about 1½ hours. Drain and pat dry.

In a bowl, whisk together ¾ cup of the balsamic vinegar and olive oil. Brush mixture on all sides of the ribs.

Season the ribs with salt and pepper. Rub both sides with garlic and rosemary. Cover tightly and marinate in the refrigerator at least 6 hours or up to 24.

Thoroughly mix remaining ½ cup of balsamic vinegar with honey. Reserve.

For the Grill: Prepare barbecue for medium heat. Arrange ribs on the rack and grill until tender and cooked through, turning occasionally, about 30 to 35 minutes. Brush each side generously with the reserved honey mixture. Continue grilling until ribs are cooked through and sauce forms a sticky coating, about 4 minutes per side. Transfer to a platter. Cut ribs between bones and serve. Cutting between each rib is important to create an enjoyable eating experience.

For the Smoker: Prepare smoker for 225 degrees. Place ribs in smoker—using a fruit wood is preferred. Cook for about 3 hours until tender but not falling off the bone. Brush generously with the reserved honey mixture and cut between the ribs.

Makes six to eight servings

Grilled Lamb Sausages

This recipe used lamb sausages from Border Springs Lamb Farm. They are delicious grilled or baked, served for breakfast along with eggs, or for dinner. In this case, try one of the sausages from La Divisa Meats, which should work equally well in the dish.

2 tablespoons olive oil

2 onions, sliced

2 red bell peppers, sliced

1 fennel bulb, sliced

Salt and pepper to taste

2 12-ounce packages lamb sausages
(any variety)

Preheat oven to 350 degrees or preheat the grill.

In a skillet, heat the oil and add the onions, peppers and fennel. Sauté until vegetables are cooked. Set aside.

To bake the sausages, place in ovenproof skillet and cook for about 10 to 15 minutes, turning them once or twice until nicely browned and cooked through.

To grill the sausages, place directly on the rack and cook for 10 to 15 minutes, turning the sausages over until nicely browned.

Add sausages to the vegetables, heat through and serve.

Makes four servings

Irina Smith's Asian Chicken Salad

During my travels to Southeast Asia, I came across many different ways of preparing this popular salad. This is my version. It can also be made with shrimp or scallops. All the ingredients are available at the Reading Terminal Market.

VINAIGRETTE

¼ cup soy sauce

2 tablespoons rice wine vinegar

2 tablespoons Asian sesame oil

1 tablespoon Dijon mustard

1 tablespoon ginger, peeled and grated

1 teaspoon dried hot pepper flakes

SALAD

4 cups (about 1 pound) coarsely chopped cooked chicken

3½ cups (about ½ pound) Napa cabbage, shredded

¼ pound snow peas, cut diagonally

1 seedless cucumber, quartered lengthwise and cut into ½-inch pieces

3 scallions, finely chopped

¼ cup cilantro, chopped

To make vinaigrette, in a bowl large enough to hold all the salad ingredients, whisk together the soy sauce, rice wine vinegar, sesame oil, Dijon mustard, ginger and pepper flakes until well combined.

Toss the prepared chicken and remaining ingredients in with the vinaigrette. Mix until well combined. Serve at room temperature.

Makes four to six servings

Irina Smith's Pork Loin with Lemongrass and Soy Sauce

I developed this recipe many years ago, when I was part of a dinner group. I have made this dish many times, especially for parties. Lemongrass is an interesting ingredient, once hard to find but now readily available, used as flavoring to accent sauces, soups and marinades. Slice very thin and chop before adding to other ingredients.

1 pork loin, 3½ to 4 pounds
¼ cup soy sauce
1 tablespoon lemon juice
1 tablespoon honey
2 tablespoons chopped lemongrass
3 garlic cloves, chopped
½ tablespoon chopped fresh ginger

1½ cups chicken stock
Zest of 1 lemon
1 red bell pepper, thinly sliced
1 scallion, chopped
¼ cup water chestnuts, sliced
1½ tablespoons cornstarch
1 teaspoon sesame oil

Place pork in a shallow pan. In a bowl, combine soy sauce, lemon juice, honey, lemongrass, ginger and half the garlic. Pour over pork and refrigerate for 4 to 6 hours. Remove 30 minutes before cooking.

Preheat oven to 350 degrees.

Remove pork from marinade and place in a roasting pan. Pour a little of the marinade over the pork and roast for approximately 2 hours. Add remaining marinade and cook another 15 to 20 minutes, or until pork is cooked through. Remove pork and keep warm.

To the pan juices, add ¼ cup of the chicken stock, lemon zest, red pepper, scallion, water chestnuts and remaining garlic, and cook about 5 minutes. Mix cornstarch into remaining chicken stock and stir into sauce. Add sesame oil and cook until sauce is slightly thickened. Slice the pork and serve with the sauce on the side.

Makes six servings

Lamb Puttanesca

Craig Rogers, owner of Border Springs Lamb Farm, told us that this is one of his favorite dishes to serve visitors to the farm and at dinner parties. It's easy to make ahead of time, and the flavors are full and rich. Craig serves this dish over penne pasta and adds fresh goat cheese as a topping. This recipe is easily made in a crock pot. Just brown the meat, add all the ingredients and go about your day. Eight hours later, you have a fabulous lamb ragout. The sauce improves by mellowing for a day or two, and can be frozen for up to 3 months.

2 to 4 lamb necks or 4 lamb shanks, about 3½ pounds
Salt
Freshly ground black pepper
2 tablespoons olive oil
1 large yellow onion, chopped
3 medium carrots, trimmed and cut into ½-inch cubes
6 large garlic cloves, chopped
1 teaspoon crushed red pepper flakes
2 tablespoons anchovy paste, or 5 anchovy fillets, drained and coarsely chopped

¾ cup coarsely chopped pitted black Kalamata or cured olives
Leaves from 3 sprigs marjoram or oregano
1 cup dry red wine, such as pinot noir
2 cups lamb broth or low-sodium beef broth
1 28-ounce can whole tomatoes and juice, crushed
2 pounds penne or other pasta choice
Chopped parsley for garnish

Season the lamb necks or shanks generously with salt and pepper.

Heat the oil in a large Dutch oven over medium-high heat until the oil shimmers. Add the necks or shanks and sear on all sides for a couple of minutes until golden brown. Transfer to a plate.

Add the onions, carrots, garlic and crushed red pepper flakes to the Dutch oven. Reduce the heat to medium and cook for about 6 minutes, stirring a few times, until the onion starts to brown. Add the anchovy paste, olives, marjoram or oregano and the red wine. Cook for 5 to 7 minutes, so most of the wine evaporates, then stir in the broth and tomatoes.

Return the necks or shanks and any accumulated juices to the pot, nestling the lamb in the sauce. Increase the heat to medium-high and bring to a boil, then reduce the heat to medium-low, cover and cook for 2 to 2½ hours, until the meat comes off the bone easily. (Turn the necks or shanks over after an hour of cooking.) Remove from heat. Transfer the lamb to a large bowl to cool.

Cook pasta in a large saucepan following package directions.

Once the necks or shanks are cool enough to handle, pull the meat from the bones, discarding any fat (you should have about 3½ cups of pulled meat). Separate the meat into bite-size pieces and return it to the sauce. Adjust the seasoning as needed. Serve over penne and garnish with parsley.

Makes 10 servings

The shop once operated by Border Springs Lamb Farm
is now occupied by La Divisa Meats.

Marita's Choucroute Garni

Although Siegfried's & Son German Gourmet is no longer at the Market, we wanted to include this recipe, which came from Marita Maldener, Siegfried's wife. Today, you can find a selection of German sausages and specialty items at Wursthaus Schmitz in the Market.

¼ pound bacon, diced
1 large onion, chopped
2 pounds fresh sauerkraut
3½ cups dry white wine
6 juniper berries, lightly crushed
2 bay leaves
1 Granny Smith apple, peeled, cored
   and chopped

4 smoked pork chops
2 links bratwurst
2 links knockwurst
2 links smoked mettwurst
2 wieners (German frankfurters)

In a large saucepan or Dutch oven, cook the bacon until lightly crisp. Add onion and sauté until soft, about 5 minutes. Add sauerkraut, wine, juniper berries, bay leaves and apple, and stir to combine. Bring mixture to a boil. Reduce heat to a simmer, cover and cook 1½ hours.

Add smoked pork chops and all the sausage links. Cover and continue simmering for another 20 minutes.

Remove sausages and cut into approximately 2-inch lengths. Place sauerkraut on a large platter and top with pork chops and sausage pieces. Serve.

Makes four servings

Market Customer: Eileen Etchells

Native-born Philadelphian Eileen Etchells walks from her 6th Street townhouse to the Reading Terminal Market to shop. Her visits always include a stop at Godshall's Poultry. Here is one of her recipes, a great entertaining dish that uses boneless chicken breasts.

Cheese-Stuffed Chicken Breasts

¾ cup cream cheese
⅓ cup blue cheese
5 tablespoons butter
Pinch of grated nutmeg
¾ cup grated Swiss cheese
4 chicken breasts skinned and boned

2 tablespoons Dijon mustard
1 egg, beaten
⅓ cup flour
¼ cup stale bread crumbs
¼ cup olive oil

Bring the cream cheese, blue cheese and butter to room temperature. Place in a bowl, and blend together until smooth. Add nutmeg and form into six ovals. Place the grated Swiss cheese on a plate and roll each oval in the cheese. Chill for at least 1 hour.

Butterfly chicken breasts and lightly flatten between sheets of wax paper. Spread the breasts with the Dijon mustard. Place a cheese oval in the center of each breast and enclose it completely with the chicken.

In three separate bowls, place the egg, flour and bread crumbs. Roll each chicken breast in the flour, then in the beaten egg and finally in the bread crumbs. Place chicken on a plate and chill for about 1 hour.

Preheat oven to 400 degrees.

In a heavy, ovenproof skillet, heat the olive oil and sear the chicken breasts for 2 to 3 minutes, or until lightly browned. Transfer the skillet to the oven and bake for about 8 to 10 minutes.

Makes four servings

Market Customer: Marge Nichols

Marge Nichols has called the Philadelphia area home since 1974. Career changes have taken her to many other cities, but she always returns to the Market when in Philadelphia. Each place she visited exposed her to unique regional and ethnic cuisines. For this recipe, you can find all the needed ingredients at the Market. Garam masala is a mix usually made from cardamom seeds, cumin seeds, whole clove, black pepper, nutmeg and cinnamon. You can buy prepared garam masala at the Head Nut.

Roast Chicken with Yogurt Masala

MARINADE
3 tablespoons plain yogurt
3 to 4 garlic cloves, minced
2 teaspoons minced ginger root
⅛ teaspoon red food coloring, optional
1 teaspoon dried coriander
2 teaspoons cumin powder
1 tablespoon lemon juice
¼ teaspoon garam masala

1 teaspoon salt, or to taste
Butter for baking
Lemon slices for garnish
Chutney for garnish
Sliced onions for garnish

2 pounds chicken parts (breasts, legs and thighs), skinned, washed and dried

Preheat oven to 350 degrees.

Make the marinade by mixing together, in a large bowl, the yogurt, garlic, ginger, food coloring (if using), coriander, cumin and lemon juice. Place chicken parts in the marinade, making sure they are well covered. Refrigerate for 4 to 5 hours or overnight. Remove from refrigerator about 30 minutes before cooking.

Place chicken parts in a frying pan and cook for about 10 minutes, turning once, to dry the excess liquids. Remove from heat and sprinkle chicken with garam masala and salt.

Line a baking sheet with buttered foil, place the chicken on the foil and dab each piece with a bit of butter. Bake for 20 to 25 minutes. Garnish with lemon slices, chutney and sliced onion.

Makes four servings

Shoppers at 10th Avenue in the Market.

Market Customer: Ronnie Colcher

Ronnie Colcher, a Center City resident, has been a Market patron for over 40 years. With pork belly gaining popularity, Ronnie wanted to make it for herself. A visit to L. Halteman Family Country Foods assured her that not only could she readily get the cut she needed for the recipe, but she could get it scored with small diamond shapes for easy preparation. Ronnie has made this dish at gatherings of family and friends, at office parties and once for a wedding celebration. "Even those who are not crazy about pork," she says, "after tasting this, come back for more."

Crispy Pork Belly

RUB
2 tablespoons black bean paste
1 tablespoon Chinese five-spice
  powder
2 teaspoons Chinese hot chili oil or
  hot sauce
1 teaspoon black pepper
1 2- to 3-pound pork belly, scored
  with small diamonds

1 tablespoon rice wine vinegar or
  white vinegar
1 tablespoon salt

DIPPING SAUCE
⅓ cup soy sauce
¼ teaspoon red chili flakes

To make rub, mix together black bean paste, five-spice powder, hot chili oil and black pepper. Rub pork belly thoroughly with mixture. Place pork belly in zip-lock bag. Refrigerate 48 hours, turning occasionally.

Preheat oven to 425 degrees.

Remove from bag and pat dry with paper towels. Place rack on top of baking sheets lined with parchment. Place pork on rack and brush top of meat with vinegar, then sprinkle with salt. Bake for ½ hour, reduce temperature to 350 degrees and cook another ½ hour. Cool and cut into bite-size pieces. Gently rewarm in the oven, and serve on toothpicks.

If using dipping sauce, combine ingredients and serve alongside.

Makes 40 serving pieces

Market Customer: Zoe Tripolitis

Zoe is a native Philadelphian who has lived in the Fitler Square neighborhood for over 15 years. She's at the Market at least twice a week to shop for poultry, meat, sausages and produce at her favorite merchant stands. "While there," she says, "I also can't resist a rib sandwich for lunch from The Rib Stand. She loves making this chicken salad using fresh ingredients, all of which are available at the Market.

Summer Chicken Salad with Apples and Grapes

DRESSING
1 cup mayonnaise
Juice 1 lemon
1 teaspoon red wine vinegar
Salt and pepper to taste

2 stalks celery
1 yellow pepper
1 large Granny Smith apple
½ red onion, diced

2 medium carrots, grated
½ cup seedless grapes, halved
1 whole chicken breast, poached
    and cubed
1 cup cooked rotini pasta
Lettuce leaves for serving
¼ cup crumbled blue cheese,
    optional
¼ cup chopped walnuts, optional

To make the dressing, in a bowl, mix together mayonnaise, lemon juice, vinegar, salt and pepper.

Chop celery, pepper and apple into bite-sized pieces. In a large bowl, combine onion, carrots and grapes with celery, pepper and apple. Add chicken and pasta to bowl. Add dressing and toss lightly. Serve on a bed of lettuce topped with blue cheese and walnuts, if desired.

Makes four to six servings

Bittersweet chocolate chip cookies with sea salt and dried cherries from Metropolitan Bakery *(see page 5).*

ABOVE: Elvis Cake from the Flying Monkey (see page 9). Photo by Albert Yee.

LEFT: Pumpkin walnut muffins from Metropolitan Bakery (see pages 18–19).

RIGHT: Bleu des Causses
from Jack Morgan of
Downtown Cheese
(see page 30).

BELOW: Ann Hazan's
pasta alla Norma *(see
page 32)*.

LEFT: Ice cream slider, a collaboration by Bassetts Ice Cream, Chocolate By Mueller and Beiler's Donuts and Salads *(see page 40).*

BELOW: Sweet sheep grilled cheese from Meltkraft at Valley Shepherd Creamery *(see pages 43–44).*

Mexican Turkey Lasagna

When Sonny Halteman, owner of A.A. Halteman, was at the Market, he suggested making lasagna with ground turkey or chicken, and using tortillas instead of the traditional lasagna pasta. This recipe was in our first *Reading Terminal Market Cookbook*.

1 pound ground turkey
8 ears fresh corn, shucked, or 1 9-ounce can whole corn, drained
1 15-ounce can tomato sauce, or homemade
1 cup picante sauce, more for serving, optional
1 tablespoon chili powder
2 garlic cloves, crushed
8 ounces cottage cheese

2 eggs, beaten
¼ cup freshly grated Parmesan cheese
1 teaspoon dried oregano
1 teaspoon dried basil
Pinch salt
12 corn tortillas
1 cup (4 ounces) shredded cheddar cheese

Preheat oven to 375 degrees.

Grease a 13 × 9 × 2-inch baking pan.

In a nonstick skillet, brown the turkey and drain any fat that has accumulated in the skillet. Add corn, tomato sauce, picante sauce, chili powder and garlic. Mix well. Simmer over low heat for about 5 minutes, stirring frequently, and set aside.

In a bowl, combine cottage cheese, eggs, Parmesan cheese, oregano, basil and salt. Mix well.

In the baking pan, arrange six of the tortillas on the bottom, overlapping as necessary. Top with half the meat mixture, then spoon the cheese mixture over the meat. Arrange the remaining tortillas over the cheese, and top with the remaining mixture.

Bake for about 30 minutes, or until hot and bubbly. Remove and sprinkle with the shredded cheddar cheese. Let stand for 10 minutes before serving. Serve with additional picante sauce, if desired.

Makes eight servings

Pan-Seared Steak Pizzaiola

Charles Giunta Jr., former owner of Giunta's Prime Shop, recommends serving this dish with rice or pasta. The recipe makes a good amount of tomato gravy, so have lots of bread handy for dunking.

2 pounds sirloin steak, cut into ¼-inch-thick slices (12 to 14 pieces)
Salt and pepper to taste
½ teaspoon garlic powder
¼ cup olive oil

3 large garlic cloves, chopped
2 16-ounce can crushed tomatoes
1½ teaspoon dried oregano
¼ teaspoon dried crushed red pepper

Sprinkle steaks on both sides with salt, pepper and garlic powder.

In a large, heavy skillet, heat olive oil over medium-high heat. Add sliced steaks (about five slices at a time). Sauté about 3 minutes per side, or to desired doneness. Transfer meat to platter. Repeat with remainder of meat.

To skillet, add garlic and sauté briefly. Add tomatoes and stir in oregano and crushed red pepper. Cover pan, reduce heat and let sauce simmer for about 20 minutes, stirring occasionally. Season with salt and pepper.

Return steaks and any juices on platter to tomato sauce and simmer on low heat for an additional 10 minutes.

Remove steaks from pan and serve along with tomato gravy.

Makes four to six servings

Pasta with Meat Gravy

This hearty pasta recipe from Martin's Quality Meats & Sausages is made with a combination of meats and produces an incredibly tasty sauce. "We call it gravy," says owner Martin Giunta, following a South Philadelphia tradition.

SAUCE

¼ cup olive oil

1 medium onion, finely chopped

3 garlic cloves, thinly sliced

4 basil leaves, coarsely chopped

2 28-ounce cans crushed tomatoes

1 can water (using tomato can)

Salt and freshly ground pepper to taste

MEATS

3 to 4 tablespoons olive oil

¼ pound each lean shoulder cuts of beef, veal and pork cut into 2-inch cubes

2 garlic cloves, minced

Salt and freshly ground pepper to taste

½ pound Italian sausage (hot or mild), cut into 3-inch pieces

MEATBALLS

½ pound each ground beef, veal and pork

2 large eggs

¼ cup grated Locatelli Romano cheese

1 cup bread crumbs (homemade are best)

2 tablespoons finely chopped Italian flat-leaf parsley

2 to 3 tablespoons olive oil

PASTA

2 pounds of spaghetti, fettucine or penne.

To make sauce, heat oil in a large saucepan over medium heat. Add onion, garlic and basil, and cook until onion has softened, about 2 minutes. Add tomato, water, salt and pepper, and simmer for approximately 10 minutes. Set aside.

To cook meats, heat oil in a large skillet and brown the beef, veal and pork cubes, turning them often. Add garlic and season with salt and pepper. Add mixture to sauce. Add sausage to skillet and brown thoroughly. Add cooked sausage to sauce.

To make meatballs, thoroughly combine all the meatball ingredients in a bowl. Form into balls about 1½ inches in diameter. Heat oil in a skillet and brown the meatballs. Add to sauce.

To finish sauce, after the meats, sausage and meatballs have been added, simmer the entire mixture for approximately 1½ hours.

Cook your favorite pasta in a large pot, following package directions. Time the pasta to be finished at the same time as the sauce. Place pasta in bowls and ladle "gravy" on top.

Makes eight to 10 servings

Chris Root displaying some of the offerings at Martin's Quality Meats & Sausages.

Roast Boned Leg of Lamb with Rosemary and White Wine

Harry Ochs always had good suggestions about cooking various cuts of meats. This was one of his recipes. He always used to say that using fresh herbs permeates the lamb and results in a juicy, succulent roast. Also, he suggested bringing the meat to room temperature before cooking to cut down on the cooking time.

MARINADE
¼ cup olive oil
1 cup dry white wine
4 garlic cloves, mashed
½ cup chopped flat-leaf parsley

2 whole sprigs rosemary
1 teaspoon freshly ground pepper

1 leg of lamb, boned and rolled,
   about 4½ to 5 pounds

To make the marinade, in a bowl, combine the olive oil, wine, garlic, parsley, rosemary and pepper. Place the lamb in a plastic bag and pour in the marinade. Seal bag, place in a shallow pan and refrigerate for 6 to 8 hours, turning the bag over once or twice.

About 30 minutes before cooking, remove lamb from refrigerator and bring to room temperature.

Preheat oven to 350 degrees.

Remove lamb and rosemary sprigs from marinade and place meat in a roasting pan. Pour some of the marinade over the lamb. Cook, uncovered, for approximately 1½ hours for rare, or 2 hours for medium, basting occasionally with reserved marinade. A thermometer inserted into the center of the lamb should register 140 degrees for rare and 160 degrees for medium. During cooking, add water to the pan as needed to prevent drippings from drying out.

Remove from oven. Place lamb on a platter and allow to rest 5 to 10 minutes before slicing. Bring pan juices to a boil along with any juices that may have accumulated on the platter and serve with the lamb.

Makes six to eight servings

Roast Quail with Port Sauce

For a delicious change of pace, try this recipe from the Frankenfields, owners of Godshall's Poultry. This dish uses a wonderful combination of figs, orange juice and port wine.

PORT SAUCE

1 cup port wine
½ cup orange juice
3 tablespoons lemon juice
1 shallot, finely chopped
½ garlic clove, minced
¼ teaspoon dried thyme
1 dried fig, chopped

QUAIL

8 whole quail, boned if desired
¼ teaspoon salt
1 tablespoon garlic powder
1 tablespoon black pepper
1 teaspoon cayenne pepper
1 teaspoon paprika
8 bacon slices

STUFFING

6 slices bacon, diced
1 small onion, chopped
1 garlic clove, minced
¼ cup port wine
2 dried figs, chopped
⅓ cup fresh bread crumbs
Salt and ground pepper to taste

To make sauce, place port wine, orange juice, lemon juice, shallot, garlic and thyme in a small saucepan and bring to a boil. Continue boiling until reduced by half and somewhat thickened, about 10 minutes. Add the chopped fig, return mixture to a boil, reduce heat, and let simmer for 1 minute. Cool and refrigerate until needed.

To make stuffing, in a large skillet over medium heat, sauté the bacon until lightly browned. Do not overcook. Reduce heat to low, add the onion and garlic and cook until onion is translucent, about 10 minutes. Add port wine and figs, increase heat, bring mixture to a low boil and cook for 2 to 3 minutes. Add bread crumbs, mix well and season with salt and pepper. Set aside.

Preheat oven to 375 degrees.

Fill each quail with an equal amount of stuffing. Combine the salt, garlic powder, black pepper, cayenne and paprika, and lightly roll each quail in the seasoning mixture. Drape a bacon strip around each quail. Place quail in a roasting pan and cook for 12 minutes.

Set oven to broil. Preheat reserved port sauce. Remove quail from oven and broil until lightly browned. Quail are done when juices run clear in thigh. Do not overcook. Spoon a portion of port sauce on each of four serving plates and place two quail on top. Serve immediately.

Makes four servings

Sausage Smothered in Onions and Tomatoes

Martin Giunta's mother, Martina, had given us one of her sausage recipes for our first Market cookbook. This dish makes excellent use of the many varieties of sausages available at Martin's Quality Meats.

3 tablespoons olive oil
2 cups onion, thinly sliced
2 cups canned Italian plum
    tomatoes, chopped

Salt and freshly ground pepper to
    taste
1 pound sausage (any variety)

Put the oil in a medium skillet, then add the onions. Cover and cook over low heat until the onion softens, about 5 minutes. Uncover and continue cooking over low heat, stirring occasionally, until onion has turned a deep golden color, about 15 minutes.

Add the tomato, salt and pepper. Reduce heat and simmer for about 20 minutes. With a fork, prick the sausages in several places and add whole to the tomato mixture. Cover the skillet and cook over medium heat for about 20 minutes, turning the sausage from time to time to cook evenly. Slice sausage and serve with sauce.

Makes four servings

Scrapple

Traditionally a breakfast food, scrapple is typically served with eggs and warm maple syrup. People are generally misinformed about scrapple. It has less fat than many think, and because of the cornmeal and buckwheat flour, it is nutritious. Perfectly cooked scrapple should have a crisp crust on the top and bottom, and a soft center. Christian Moyer developed this recipe in 1856 when he opened Moyer's, which then became Eugene M. Moyer & Son. Although the Moyer stand is no longer in the Market, scrapple is still available at Quality Meats, Smucker's and L. Halteman Family Country Foods.

1 meaty pork neck bone, cut into 2-inch pieces	Water
1½ pounds pork cubes from shoulder	½ cup cornmeal
½ pound pork trimmings	Salt and freshly ground pepper to taste
½ pound pork liver	¼ cup buckwheat flour
	Vegetable oil for frying

Place pork neck bone, pork cubes, pork trimmings and pork liver into a large saucepan and cover with approximately 6 cups of water. Bring to a boil, reduce heat and simmer for 1½ hours. When meat is very tender, remove from broth, strain the broth and pour 3½ cups of it back into the saucepan. Reserve remaining broth.

Remove meat from neck bones. In the bowl of a food processor fitted with the steel blade, combine all the meats and process until coarsely ground.

Over low heat, gradually pour the cornmeal into broth, stirring constantly until smooth, approximately 10 minutes. Add the ground meat to the cooked cornmeal and stir to mix. Season with salt and pepper.

Add buckwheat flour to the mixture and cook for about 10 minutes, or until thickened. Pour mixture into loaf pan. Cool for 30 minutes and refrigerate for 24 hours.

Remove from refrigerator and cut into ⅜-inch slices. In a large skillet, heat oil until hot, and pan-fry scrapple in batches over medium heat for about 10 minutes on one side, until nicely browned and crisp. Turn and cook about 5 minutes on the other side. Serve.

Makes six to eight servings

Smoked Ham "Paté"

Eugene M. Moyer & Son developed this recipe using leftover ends of smoked ham that became a very popular item. Over the years, we have made this "paté" using other smoked meats, such as chicken and duck. It is delicious spread over bagels, as a sandwich filling or on crackers for hors d'oeuvres.

1 pound smoked ham
2 hard-cooked eggs
½ cup sweet gherkins, with juice
1 tablespoon prepared mustard

⅓ cup pitted black olives
¾ cup sandwich spread or
   mayonnaise

Place the ham into a food processor or blender, and mix until just ground. Add remaining ingredients and blend until smooth.

Makes three cups

Stuffed Cornish Game Hens

Holiday season is an exciting time at the Market. Customers line up at their favorite meat and poultry stand to order or pick up their turkey, goose, duck or game hens for their festive family dinner. Cornish hens can be prepared in less than two hours and make an impressive presentation for any gathering.

4 Cornish game hens
1 orange
12 tablespoons (1½ sticks) unsalted
    butter
½ cup minced onion
½ cup minced celery
½ teaspoon dried thyme, additional
    for hens
½ teaspoon dried marjoram,
    additional for hens
teaspoon sage, additional for hens
2 very small Granny Smith apples,
    cored and finely diced

⅓ cup golden raisins
2 tablespoons minced flat-leaf parsley
1½ cups cubed bread
    (preferably from an Italian or
    French loaf)
1 tablespoon toasted pine nuts,
    optional
Salt and freshly ground pepper to
    taste
¼ cup white wine (dry vermouth
    may be used)
¼ cup chicken broth, additional as
    needed

Preheat oven to 350 degrees.

Rinse hens in cold water inside and out. Pat dry thoroughly.

Grate zest of orange. Set aside. Cut orange in half and rub outside of hens.

In a skillet, over medium-low heat, melt 6 tablespoons of the butter and sauté onion and celery until soft. Add thyme, marjoram and sage. Set aside.

In a bowl, combine diced apples, raisins, parsley, cubed bread, reserved orange zest and pine nuts, if using. Add the onion mixture, season with salt and pepper and toss to combine.

Distribute stuffing evenly and spoon into hen cavity. Tie legs together with kitchen string and tuck wing tips under body of hens. Place in a shallow roasting pan. Melt remaining 6 tablespoons of butter and brush over hens. Season with thyme, marjoram, sage, salt and pepper. Add white wine and broth to pan and roast for about 1 to

1½ hours, or until golden brown and tender. Add additional broth to pan as needed. Baste hens occasionally during cooking. Remove from oven and let rest about 10 minutes before serving.

Makes four servings

Turkey Chili

Here is a hearty recipe from Godshall's Poultry, using their ground turkey. This is a wonderful, spicy chili to make during the cold winter months.

1 tablespoons olive oil
2 medium onions, diced
2 tablespoons, garlic, minced
1 green bell pepper, diced
1 red bell pepper, diced
1 teaspoon jalapeño pepper, minced
3 pounds fresh ground turkey
2 tablespoons chili powder
½ teaspoon ground coriander
Pinch ground cinnamon
½ teaspoon cayenne pepper
1½ teaspoons oregano

1 teaspoon salt
1½ teaspoons mustard powder
2 15-ounce cans dark red kidney beans, drained and rinsed
1 28-ounce can crushed tomatoes
1 can of dark beer
½ cup chopped parsley
½ cup pitted black olives, sliced
Sour cream, sliced scallions and grated cheddar cheese for garnish, optional

Heat oil in a large saucepan over medium heat. Add onion, garlic, red and green bell peppers and jalapeño pepper. Cook and stir for 5 minutes. Add ground turkey and brown with vegetables. When browned, drain off any excess liquid.

Add the chili powder, coriander, cinnamon, cayenne pepper, oregano, salt, mustard powder, beans, tomatoes, beer, parsley and olives. Simmer over medium-low heat for 30 minutes. Do not boil.

Serve with sour cream, scallions and cheddar cheese, if desired.

Makes eight servings

Turkey London Broil with Beer and Honey

Butterflied turkey breast, which Godshall's Poultry markets as "turkey London broil," is easy to prepare and a healthy alternative to the traditional version made with beef. When using a marinade for a sauce, remember to bring the juices to a boil in a separate saucepan, and simmer for at least 5 minutes to kill any bacteria that may have accumulated.

MARINADE
1 cup honey
2 tablespoons chopped fresh sage,
    or 1 tablespoon dried
2 teaspoons chili powder
1½ teaspoons dry mustard

2 tablespoons fresh lemon juice
Salt to taste
3 cups beer

1 turkey London broil, 2 to 2½
    pounds

In a bowl, combine honey, sage, chili powder, dry mustard, lemon juice and salt. Slowly pour in the beer and whisk until all ingredients are well combined.

Place the meat in a shallow pan and pour the marinade on top. Refrigerate 6 to 8 hours, turning several times to coat evenly with the marinade.

Set oven to broil.

To cook, remove turkey from pan and reserve the marinade. Place the turkey on a broiler pan and broil about 4 inches from the heat source for 15 to 20 minutes, or until cooked through. Turn several times during cooking and baste with reserved marinade.

To serve, cut the turkey in thin slices against the grain. Pour any remaining marinade into a saucepan, bring to a boil and simmer for about 5 minutes. Serve alongside.

Makes four servings

Seafood
Merchants

FRESHNESS IS THE key to the enjoyment of seafood, and there is no better place to buy it than the Reading Terminal Market. We are fortunate to live in a part of the country that has access to local fish and shellfish. In the spring, we can find shad and shad roe. There are oysters and mussels for most of the year as well as soft-shell crabs and hard-shell crabs, also known as blue crabs, during the summer months. Many other local fish are available, including rockfish, bluefish, trout and perch. You will also find seafood from around the country and the world, such as red snapper and rock lobster from Florida and the Caribbean, scrod and cold-water lobster from Maine, sashimi-grade tuna from Hawaii, St. Peter's fish from Israel and salmon from Norway and Canada. All these fish and many more can be found at any of the three fish stalls at the Market.

All the merchants agree that when buying whole fish, one foolproof way of determining its freshness is to see if the eyes are clear and bright, but never cloudy. Fish should smell fresh and mild, not "fishy" or faintly like ammonia. To store fish, they recommend unwrapping it as soon as possible, placing it in a shallow bowl on a bed of ice, covering it with plastic wrap and storing it in the refrigerator. Fresh fish should be used within 24 hours of buying. If previously frozen, it should not be placed in the freezer. When cooking fish, timing is everything. Doneness can be tested by pressing the fish gently. If properly done, the fish should feel almost firm and

A selection of seafood at the Market.

the center should be opaque. The usual timing is 8 to 10 minutes per inch of thickness. For shellfish such as mussels, clams and oysters, the shells should open during cooking; throw out ones that remain closed. All of the fish stalls at the Market have staff that is knowledgeable and willing to answer questions from customers.

Rosa and Leo Kong, owners of Golden Fish Market, sell a large selection of fresh and prepared fish. They carry clams, live and cooked crabs and live lobsters, as well as smelts, fresh sardines, cooked crawfish and spiced jumbo shrimp. Other specialties include Scottish smoked salmon, New Zealand green mussels and frog legs.

"Eat Fish and Live Longer" proclaims the sign above John Yi Fish Market, now owned by Suzi Kim. A vast array of fish and shellfish are displayed on ice. Among their most popular items are sushi-grade ahi tuna, wild sockeye salmon, frozen lobster tails and king crabs. Customers also can choose live lobsters from their glass tank.

Wan Woo, owner of Wan's Seafood, bought and took over Byun's Seafood, where they continue to carry fresh fish and shellfish and fish to go. Their display counters are full of fresh fish, jumbo shrimp, "dry" scallops, seasonal soft shell crabs and much more. At the takeout counter, the lunch crowd lines up to buy Wan's crispy fried clams by the basketful. You can also find breaded flounder, hand-formed crab and fish cakes, shrimp and scallops, both ready to eat at the Market or to take home.

Past Merchants of the Market

Many Reading Terminal Market customers will remember the Philadelphia Lobster & Fish Company, best known for its glass tank filled with lobsters and gigantic Dungeness crabs. Steven Cho took over the business and renamed it Coastal Cave Trading Company, but Steven continued to supply Market customers with the same seafood selections until he retired in 2012. Recipes from Philadelphia Lobster & Fish Company remain in this new edition of *The Reading Terminal Market Cookbook*.

Ann Hazan's Scallops with Quinoa and Mango

I use sea scallops for this recipe, but smaller bay scallops work just as well, and they require less cooking time. Regardless of which you choose, the freshest selection of scallops is available at any of the three fish stands at the Market: Golden Fish Market, John Yi Fish Market and Wan's Seafood.

QUINOA AND MANGO
1 cup quinoa, rinsed and drained
1½ cups low-sodium chicken broth
¼ teaspoon garlic powder
½ teaspoon curry powder
½ teaspoon salt
Freshly ground pepper to taste
1 mango, peeled and diced
3 green onions, finely chopped

SCALLOPS
2 tablespoons olive oil
12 sea scallops, rinsed and patted
    dry
Salt and freshly ground pepper to
    taste
Juice of ½ lemon

To make quinoa and mango, in a saucepan, combine quinoa, broth, garlic powder, curry powder, salt and pepper. Bring to a boil. Reduce heat to simmer. Cover and cook about 15 to 20 minutes, then fluff with a fork. Place in a bowl. Toss in mango and onions, and set aside.

In a skillet that will hold scallops comfortably, heat oil until hot but not smoking. Sauté scallops until golden on both sides, about 3 to 4 minutes per side (scallops should be white in center). Season with salt and pepper.

To serve, distribute quinoa and mango evenly between four plates and serve scallops alongside. Sprinkle scallops with lemon juice and serve.

Makes four servings

Baked Salmon with Mediterranean Tapenade

Salmon is a popular fish, rich in omega-3 fatty acids. Varieties of salmon are available at any of the fish stalls in the Market. The merchants carry wild king salmon, Norwegian and Scottish salmon, wild coho and Atlantic salmon. Salmon steaks can be substituted for fillets. The intense flavor of capers and olives complements the richness of the salmon.

1½ to 2 pounds boned salmon fillets
2 tablespoons olive oil
1 tablespoon lemon juice
1 tablespoon mayonnaise
1 tablespoon Dijon mustard
4 plum tomatoes, seeded and
   chopped

1 tablespoon minced garlic
2 tablespoons chopped capers
⅓ cup pitted chopped Kalamata
   olives
⅓ cup chopped basil
Salt and pepper to taste

Preheat oven to 375 degrees.

Using tweezers, remove any pin bones from the salmon. Refrigerate fish until ready to cook.

In a small bowl, whisk together the olive oil, lemon juice, mayonnaise and mustard. Set aside.

In another bowl, combine the tomatoes, garlic, basil, capers, olives, salt and pepper to form tapenade. Set aside.

Place salmon skin side down on a lightly oiled baking sheet and brush top with the mayonnaise-mustard mixture. Bake for 2 to 4 minutes, then spoon 2 to 3 tablespoons of the tapenade over the fish. Continue cooking for another 5 to 8 minutes until fish is almost opaque throughout, but still moist. Serve with the rest of the tapenade on the side.

Makes four servings

Irina Smith's Baked Fish with Tomatoes and Olives

This tasty dish uses the wonderful supply of fresh fish from any of the fish purveyors in the Market. I often serve asparagus in season or green beans as side dishes along with warm, crusty bread.

1 tablespoon olive oil
1 tablespoon unsalted butter
1 large onion, finely sliced
2 garlic cloves, finely sliced
4 large potatoes, skin on, finely sliced
6 plum tomatoes, roughly chopped
1 cup dry white wine

2½ pounds fish (cod, halibut, sea bass or salmon), cut into 6 equal pieces
salt and pepper
1 cup chopped Italian flat-leaf parsley
½ cup pitted black olives, chopped
Fresh green peas for garnish, optional

Preheat oven to 350 degrees.

Melt the oil and butter in an ovenproof roasting pan. Add onions and cook for a few minutes, until beginning to soften. Add garlic and potatoes and mix well with the onions.

Stir in tomatoes and add the wine. Bubble rapidly until reduced by half. Roast for 20 to 25 minutes, or until the potatoes are tender and the tomatoes have softened.

Add fish to the pan, nestling it among the potatoes and tomatoes. Spoon some of the sauce over the fish and season lightly with salt and pepper. Cook 10 minutes longer, or until the fish is just cooked through. Sprinkle with parsley and olives. Garnish with green peas, if desired.

Makes six servings

Irina Smith's Baked Shad with Herbs

I always enjoy the first signs of spring in the Market with the appearance of shad. This fast-moving fish migrates with the seasons. The start of shad season in the Philadelphia area is celebrated annually at the Lambertville Shad Festival in New Jersey, about 45 minutes from Philadelphia. Shad is a rich fish with a soft flesh and fine texture, which lends itself to baking, broiling or grilling. If you don't have herbes de Provence in your cupboard, try chopped fresh or dried tarragon instead. In season, shad can be found at any of the fish stalls in the Market.

2 boneless shad fillets, each about 1 pound
¼ cup olive oil
Juice of 1 lemon
⅓ cup white wine or dry vermouth

1 tablespoon herbes de Provence
Salt and freshly ground pepper to taste
Lemon wedges for garnish

Preheat oven to 350 degrees.

Place shad, skin side down, in a shallow, ovenproof pan large enough to hold the fillets in one layer. In a bowl, mix together the olive oil, lemon juice, wine or vermouth, herbes de Provence, salt and pepper. Brush fish liberally with this mixture.

Place fish in the oven and cook for 6 to 8 minutes, basting once or twice with the oil mixture. Fish is cooked when fillets are opaque and flake easily with a fork. Pour any juices that have accumulated in the pan over the fish and adjust seasonings. Cut fillets in half, garnish with lemon wedges and serve.

Makes four servings

Irina Smith's Sautéed Soft-Shell Crabs

There are many ways of cooking soft-shell crabs, but this is one of my favorite recipes. Soft-shell crabs are hard crabs that have shed their shells. Fishermen usually catch them just as they start shedding. The crabs are put in a holding tank where they are continually monitored. As soon as they shed their shells, the crabs are immediately placed on ice. Soft shells are an East Coast delicacy and are generally available from June until September. Always purchase soft shells alive, and ask your fishmonger to clean them.

Cornstarch for dredging
Salt and pepper to taste
4 tablespoons olive oil
2 tablespoon unsalted butter
8 soft-shell crabs, cleaned and
    patted dry

Grated zest and juice of two limes
½ cup dry white wine or vermouth
Salt and freshly ground pepper to
    taste

In a bowl, combine cornstarch with the salt and pepper. Dredge crabs lightly in the cornstarch mixture and shake off excess.

Add olive oil and butter to a skillet large enough to hold crabs in one layer, or cook in batches. Heat oil and butter until sizzling hot. Gently sauté crabs for about 5 minutes on each side, or until well browned and crisped (be careful of splattering). Remove from pan and keep warm.

Add lime zest, lime juice and wine or vermouth to skillet, deglazing it by scraping up the browned bits with a wooden spoon. Season with salt and pepper. Serve crabs drizzled with sauce from skillet.

Makes four servings

Lobster Grill

This recipe came from the Philadelphia Lobster & Fish Company. Many Reading Terminal Market customers will remember their glass tank filled with lobsters and Dungeness crabs. Each year, thousands of children and adults were mesmerized by the giant crabs from the Pacific Northwest. Lobster can be purchased from any of the fish merchants in the Market.

4 live lobsters, 1¼ to 2 pounds each

MARINADE
¾ cup olive oil
⅓ cup fresh lime juice
2½ tablespoons garlic, mashed
½ cup chopped cilantro

Salt and freshly ground
   pepper to taste
Lemon wedges, optional
Clarified butter, optional

Split lobsters through head and almost through tail, enough to open wide. Wash out chest cavity and crack claws.

To make the marinade, in a bowl, combine the oil, lime juice, garlic, cilantro, salt and pepper. Set aside.

Rub marinade over lobster, allowing excess to drain off, and let sit 10 minutes.

Prepare grill or barbecue.

Grill, shell side down, for about 3 to 5 minutes. Turn over and cook another 2 minutes, or until done.

Serve with lemon wedges and/or clarified butter, if desired.

Makes four servings

Market Customer: Anonymous

Sautéed Shad Roe

Shad roe is delicate in texture yet rich in taste. Preparing the roe simply and serving with a light sauce is one of the best ways to enjoy it. One useful trick is to place the roe in warm water for a few minutes. That will help keep it firm and intact during cooking. When in season, shad roe is available at any of the three Market fish stands.

2 sets shad roe
Salt and freshly ground pepper to
 taste
½ cup flour
¼ pound (1 stick) unsalted butter
1 tablespoon olive oil

⅓ cup white wine or dry vermouth
Juice of 1 lemon
1 teaspoon champagne mustard or
 Dijon mustard
2 tablespoons chopped fennel
 leaves

Dip roe in warm water and let sit for a few minutes. Drain and pat dry with paper towel. Separate the lobes by gently removing the membrane between them. Sprinkle with salt and pepper. Dredge in flour and gently shake off excess.

In a skillet, melt 6 tablespoons of the butter with the oil. When the mixture begins to foam, reduce the heat, gently add the roe, and cook for about 5 to 6 minutes on each side. Carefully transfer to a warm platter and set aside.

In the same skillet, add remaining 2 tablespoons of butter. Stir in the wine or vermouth and lemon juice, then cook until reduced by half. Add the mustard and fennel leaves. Simmer for 1 to 2 minutes, pour sauce over roe and serve.

Makes four servings

Market Customers: Otto and Nury Reichert

This recipe came from Otto and Nury Reichert. They discovered their love of Spanish cooking while taking many vacations in Spain. When shopping in the Market, Otto enjoyed talking to the merchants. This recipe combines fish and shellfish with the flavors of Spain.

Bouillabaisse Catalana

¼ cup olive oil

3 ribs celery, finely chopped

1 medium onion, finely chopped

1 garlic clove, finely chopped

1 scallion, finely chopped

1 teaspoon dried thyme, or 1 tablespoon fresh

1 bay leaf

1 28-ounce can crushed tomatoes

3 8-ounce bottles clam juice

1 cup dry white wine

2 tablespoons fresh parsley, minced

1 bulb fennel, finely chopped

Salt and freshly ground pepper to taste

1 pound white fish (monkfish, cod or flounder), cut in chunks

½ pound medium shrimp, peeled

¾ pound bay scallops

Heat oil in a large saucepan over medium heat and sauté the celery, onion, garlic, scallion, thyme and bay leaf for about 15 minutes, stirring frequently. Add tomatoes, clam juice, wine, parsley, fennel, salt and pepper, and simmer 15 minutes longer.

Add fish chunks, shrimp and scallops to the soup and simmer about 5 minutes, or until fish, shrimp and scallops are cooked through.

Makes six to eight servings

Monkfish Soup

According to Suzi Kim, owner of John Yi Fish Market—who is of Chinese descent and supplied this recipe—Koreans also make this soup and call it Me Untang. Kimchi is a fermented Korean side dish, usually made from Napa cabbage, radish, garlic, red pepper, salt and sugar. Kimchi is available at Jonathon Best Gourmet Grocer.

1 pound monkfish or cod, cut into
    1-inch chunks
1 teaspoon miso paste
1 tablespoon soy sauce

1 garlic clove, peeled and crushed
6 cups water
½ cup kimchi

In a large saucepan, place fish, miso, soy sauce, garlic and water. Bring to a boil, reduce heat, and simmer for 8 to 10 minutes, or until fish flakes easily. Add kimchi and simmer another 2 to 3 minutes, or until just heated through.

Makes four servings

A fresh catch at the John Yi Fish Market.

Orange Roughy with Lemon Marinade and Snowpeas

Suzi Kim of John Yi Fish Market prefers simplicity in fish cookery, which is evident in the following recipe that she provided. Other types of white fish, such as flounder, can be substituted.

Grated zest of 1 lemon and juice of ½ lemon

2 teaspoons Dijon mustard

2 tablespoons olive oil

4 orange roughy fillets, about 1½ pounds total

Salt and freshly ground pepper to taste

½ pound snow peas, trimmed

Preheat oven to 350 degrees.

In a small bowl, whisk together lemon juice, lemon zest and mustard. Gradually add oil until well blended. Lightly oil a baking pan and add fish in one layer. Season with salt and pepper, then pour marinade on top.

Cover fish with foil and bake for approximately 5 minutes. Remove foil and continue baking for another 5 minutes, or until fish is opaque.

While fish is baking, bring a saucepan of water to a boil. Add snow peas and blanch for about 20 seconds. Drain peas and serve alongside.

Makes four servings

Shrimp Scampi

Quick, easy, tasty—that perfectly describes this recipe for shrimp scampi. All of the seafood merchants at the Market agree: simplicity is often best for cooking fish and shellfish. This dish is perfect as a main course with a side of greens and some crusty bread, or on top of pasta or rice. If desired, a little white wine or dry vermouth may be added to deglaze the pan after the shrimp are cooked.

4 tablespoons unsalted butter

4 tablespoons extra virgin olive oil

4 garlic cloves, minced

1 pound large shrimp, peeled and deveined

⅓ cup chopped flat-leaf parsley

Zest from ½ lemon

¼ cup freshly squeezed lemon juice

Freshly ground black pepper to taste

Dash hot red pepper flakes, optional

Place a large skillet over medium heat, combine butter and olive oil. Sauté garlic until lightly golden, about 1 minute. Add shrimp and sauté until pink, about 3 to 4 minutes, tossing often. Remove from heat, add parsley, lemon zest and lemon juice. Season with black pepper and red pepper flakes, if using. Toss to combine. Serve.

Makes four servings

Smoked Fish Spread

This recipe is from the Philadelphia Lobster & Fish Company when they were in the Reading Terminal Market. It was featured in our first Market cookbook. Smoked trout, salmon or bluefish are equally good for this tasty spread. Choose according to availability and your own preference.

8 ounces cream cheese, softened
¼ cup sour cream
3 tablespoons white horseradish

½ pound smoked fish, skin removed
　and broken into chunks
1 tablespoon lemon juice

Assorted vegetables or black bread

In a food processor or blender, combine the cream cheese, sour cream, horseradish and lemon juice until smooth. Add the fish and process just until blended. Place mixture in a bowl and serve with vegetables or black bread.

Makes about two cups

Steamed Red Snapper

There are many ways of preparing white fish. In this recipe from Golden Fish Market, red snapper is used. This simple marinade is equally delicious over other white fish. All it needs is some rice and a green vegetable.

4 red snapper fillets

MARINADE

1 teaspoon chopped ginger

2 garlic cloves, chopped

1 tablespoon oyster sauce

¼ cup rice wine vinegar

½ teaspoon hot pepper sauce

Place fish fillets in a shallow pan. In a bowl, combine remaining ingredients and pour over fish. Marinate in the refrigerator for 1 to 2 hours. Remove fish from marinade and place in a steamer.

Pour some of the marinade over the fish. Let steam about 5 minutes, or until fish is firm and opaque.

Boil remaining marinade in a small saucepan for about 5 minutes. Place fish on a platter and serve with heated sauce.

Makes four servings

Pennsylvania Dutch

ENNSYLVANIA'S HEARTLAND ARRIVED at Reading Terminal Market in 1981 when David O'Neil, then the general manager, went out to Lancaster County to personally persuade some of the local Amish and Mennonite farmer-merchants to open businesses in the Market. Now an entire corner of the building bustles with country-fresh produce and Pennsylvania Dutch specialties. The stands are family-owned and -operated, and many of the merchants are related.

Alvin Beiler, owner of Beiler's Bakery, can still be found behind the counter, greeting customers after 28 years. The bakery showcases homemade sticky buns and dinner rolls. Many of their bakery items are baked on the premises, while others come in fresh from a Mennonite bakery in nearby Lancaster County. The shelves are filled with pastries, cakes, chocolate éclairs, fruit pies, lemon meringue pies, cream pies and, of course, Pennsylvania Dutch shoofly pie. About seven years ago, the Beiler family purchased and opened another stand across the aisle: A.J. Pickle Patch & Salads (previously Glick's Salad stand). Finding the need to expand their bakery, they renovated that location and opened Beiler's Donut Shop with the Pickle Patch right next door.

Beiler's Donut Shop is new to the Market, but the Beiler name is not. Alvin Beiler has fulfilled a "donut-lover's dream" along with his two sons, Kevin and Keith, who manage the day-to-day operation. After being open only three months,

A view from the 2014 Pennsylvania Dutch Festival at the Market.
(Photo courtesy of Stephen Hoeprich.)

the shop won Best of Philly. They used to make the donuts—about five different types—from their Beiler's Bakery location, exclusively for festivals in the Market. The demand increased to the point that the family opened Beiler's Donut Shop, where they now make over 40 varieties right on the premises. You can even watch them roll out the dough. The varieties include Double Chocolate Mousse, Key Lime Pie, Pumpkin and Caramel Apple, to name only a few. According to Kevin Beiler, the most popular is still the traditional glazed, followed by the Apple Fritter. Around the corner is the Pickle Patch, where they still sell a selection of the salads and pickles once available at A.J. Pickle Patch & Salads.

Gideon Dienner started Dienner's Bar-B-Q Chicken in 1981, and the stand has quite a following to this day. His son, Sam, took over a few years later. Still keeping it in the family, Sam's son, Anthony, will eventually take charge of the business. "That's three generations of Dienners in the Market," says Sam proudly. They are well known in town for their barbequed chicken, served with or without their special hot sauce. Other best-sellers are the barbecued chicken wings and the rotisserie whole or half chickens, all served with hot dinner rolls and coleslaw.

You can enjoy home-style cooking—comfort food at its best—at the Dutch Eating Place, opened in 1990 by Sam Esh Jr. Long lines form early in the morning when breakfast eaters wait eagerly for Sam's famous pancakes served with a side of turkey bacon. The French toast is made using fresh raisin bread from nearby Beiler's Bakery. At lunch, stop by and watch them ladle out their hearty bean-and-ham soup, chicken-corn soup and chili. The Dutch Eating Place has been mentioned in *Bon Appetit* and on the Food Network for their wonderful cooking.

David Esh arrived in the Market in the early 1980s and set up Hatville Deli, specializing in quality meats and cheeses. The deli features displays of sliced sugar ham, smoked turkey, pepper ham, regular and sweet bologna, delicious slabs of bacon and much more. Hatville's selection of cheeses includes bacon-horseradish cheddar, steakhouse onion cheddar, and many other varieties. Try their whipped butter made of 60 percent butter and 40 percent margarine. Around the corner is

The Dutch Eating Place.

a sandwich counter. The menu includes their pastrami sandwich, a Philly special, along with Buffalo chicken breast and country-style ham sandwiches.

Benuel Kauffman of Kauffman's Lancaster County Produce has been a fixture in the Market since 1987. Benuel proudly told us that his youngest son, Amos, bought the stand from him recently. Now Benuel works for his son! Amos has helped his father from a very young age, so he knows the business well. The Kauffmans work directly with area farmers to bring their fruit and vegetables to the Reading Terminal Market, but they also bring in their own produce in season, including strawberries, asparagus, beets, squash, tomatoes and other seasonal favorites. Benuel's wife cans her own beets and makes her own stuffed peppers with cabbage. Kauffman's also carries sweet pepper relish, chow chow, corn relish and many preserves, jams and jellies, as well as packaged foods and Pennsylvania Dutch craft items.

L. Halteman Family Country Foods is now owned by Amos and Anna Ruth Riehl. They took over from the Haltemans about 16 years ago, and they continue to offer home-raised poultry, ducks, geese and rabbits. They also carry smoked turkey legs and spareribs, fresh-cut pork and pork shoulder roasts. Across the aisle is a display of seasonal fruits and vegetables. Two years ago, the business expanded to include Riehl's Deli, which offers a wide selection of cheeses and cream cheese spreads, such as bacon-horseradish, provolone, Chianti-cheese, pimento and apple-cinnamon-raisin. Along one side of the counter there are mounds of thinly sliced meats such as smoked turkey, smoked ham, pastrami, roast beef, and much more.

Lancaster County Dairy, owned by Samuel Esh, has been in the Market for about 20 years. They carry many different dairy products, such as farm-fresh milk, raw goat's milk, fresh organic milk and fresh buttermilk. Lancaster County Dairy also offers white and chocolate milk, as well as light and thick heavy cream, but the best-sellers are their freshly squeezed seasonal fruit juices and fresh apple cider.

Miller's Twist is owned by Roger and Shauna Miller, who live in Lancaster County with their three children. They have been in operation since 2009 after buying Fisher's Soft Pretzels & Ice Cream. Fisher's was a longtime Market business and won the Best of Philly award at least three times in the 1980s and '90s. Miller's Twist continued the tradition of producing great pretzels by winning the award in their first year at the Market in 2009.

The Grill at Smucker's and Quality Meats at Smucker's are owned by Pennsylvania Dutchman Moses Smucker, who is often found behind the counter. Moses ran a harness shop for 38 years before he decided to embark on his latest business venture in 2009. At the Grill at Smuckers, you can find a wide range of breakfast

Donut-making at the Market's 2014 Pennsylvania Dutch Festival.

sandwiches, including Amish-style sausage sandwiches and their signature pot-roast sandwich. Around the corner at Quality Meats at Smucker's, you can purchase fresh and smoked meats, including smoked ham, beef jerky, chicken, turkey, pepperoni sticks, smoked kielbasa and more.

Sweet as Fudge Candy Shoppe, as it is known today, is at the old Fisher's location. It started as Fisher's Dutch Treats and was run by John Fisher. In 1999, Levi Fisher changed the name to Fisher's Soft Pretzels & Ice Cream. Another change occurred in 2009, when Paul Fisher, Levi's son, made the business what it is today.

Sweet as Fudge makes its own variety of homemade fudge with real cream and butter in flavors like s'mores, piña colada, banana split and root beer. Many shoppers are thrilled to find traditional old-fashioned candies. Browsers will find other goodies such as nut brittle, dried fruits and assorted nuts.

Phares Glick's Rib Stand opened in early 1994. The family-run business sells large quantities of both baby-back and regular ribs, accompanied by a selection of vegetable side dishes. The potato wedges are in great demand, as are the baked macaroni and cheese and coleslaw. Not to be missed is a delectable rib sandwich, served on a club roll with hot or mild barbecue sauce.

Past Merchants of the Market

Glick's Salads occupied a place in the Market until 2007, when they were taken over by A.J. Pickle Patch and later by Beiler's Donuts. We have included one of their recipes that was featured in our original cookbook.

Esh Eggs was another stand once run by David Esh. The business was a part of the Market until 2007. Longtime customers might remember the many varieties on display, including chicken, duck and goose eggs, as well as the more exotic eggs of the ostrich, rhea and emu.

Bacon Hot Dogs

When a good basic sandwich is what you crave, that means a visit to The Grill at Smuckers. This bacon-wrapped hot dog appetizer takes us back in time, and is sure to please the kid in all of us!

10 hot dogs	Vegetable oil for greasing pan
10 slices bacon	Brown sugar to taste

Preheat oven to 400 degrees.

Slice each hot dog and bacon slice into three pieces. Wrap bacon around hot dogs and secure with toothpicks. Place onto a lightly greased 13 × 9 × 1½-inch pan. Sprinkle with brown sugar. Bake until bacon is slightly crispy. Serve at once.

Makes 30 pieces

The sign above The Grill at Smucker's.

Chicken and Corn Soup

Soups are very popular at the Dutch Eating Place. This version is especially good when local corn is available. The mixture of egg, milk and flour, when dropped into the finished soup, forms dumplings that float to the top.

1 chicken, 3 to 4 pounds	4 cups fresh or frozen corn
Water	Salt and freshly ground pepper to
1 medium onion, diced	taste
3 medium celery, diced	1 egg
3 medium potatoes, cubed	½ cup milk
1 carrot, diced	1 cup flour
¼ cup fresh parsley, chopped	

Place the chicken in a large stockpot and add enough water to cover. Bring to a boil, reduce heat to a simmer, and cook until chicken is tender, about 1 hour, adding water as needed. Remove chicken from broth and let cool. Remove and discard skin and cut the meat into 1-inch cubes. Refrigerate until ready to use. Refrigerate broth. When fat solidifies on surface, remove from refrigerator and skim off fat.

In a large saucepan, bring 8 cups of the broth to a boil. Add water if necessary to make 8 cups. Add the onion, celery, potato and carrot. Simmer covered for 30 minutes. Add the parsley and corn, and continue cooking until the vegetables are tender, about 15 minutes. Add chicken, salt and pepper.

In a small bowl, whisk egg until light in color. Beat in flour and milk until smooth. Drop batter (about 1 tablespoon) into the soup, stirring constantly for 2 to 3 minutes until dumplings hold their shape and float to the surface. Serve.

Makes four servings

Chicken Pot Pie

When the Pennsylvania Dutch mention "pot pies," they are referring to deep dishes filled with large squares of egg noodles, not to shallow dishes covered with baked pastry crust. The Dutch Eating Place is well known for serving comfort foods. When the weather is not too warm, stop in the Market and try their chicken pot pie and other hearty fare.

6 cups water
6 chicken bouillon cubes
2 tablespoons butter
1 potato (any variety), peeled and cut into ½-inch cubes
2 carrots, thinly sliced
2 ribs celery, thinly sliced

1 small onion, thinly sliced
Salt and freshly ground pepper to taste
½ pound egg noodles
2 cups cooked chicken (light or dark meat), skinned, boned and cut into 1-inch cubes

Boil the water in a large saucepan and add the bouillon cubes. Stir until cubes have dissolved. Reduce heat to medium-low and add the butter, potato, carrot, celery, onion, salt and pepper.

Add the noodles, pushing them down into the broth with a spoon. Cover and cook over low heat until noodles are done, about 25 minutes. Add the chicken and continue cooking 10 minutes longer. Adjust seasoning. Ladle into soup bowls and serve.

Makes six servings

Cole Slaw

After a long morning of shopping or meetings, many hungry people flock to The Rib Stand for great, juicy ribs with "slaw." Cole slaw goes perfectly with ribs or a barbecued rib sandwich.

1 small head green cabbage, shredded

2 carrots, grated

1 tablespoon sugar

1 tablespoon vegetable oil

2 tablespoons red wine vinegar or cider vinegar

½ teaspoon ground celery seed

Salt and freshly ground pepper to taste

1 cup mayonnaise

Place the shredded cabbage in a medium bowl and add the grated carrot, sugar, oil, vinegar, celery seed, salt and pepper. Squeeze by hand to extract and blend the juices. Add mayonnaise and mix thoroughly. Chill for 1 to 2 hours before serving.

Makes six servings

The Rib Stand, specializing in baby back ribs, sandwiches and roasted potatoes.

Creamy Fudge

You can buy different flavors of fudge at the Sweet as Fudge Candy Shoppe. Their classic fudge is made with real cream and butter. Here is a fudge recipe we discovered that is easy to make at home. A couple of tips: Use a little cooking spray on your paper lining. And when cutting the fudge, run the knife under hot water so that it won't stick to the fudge.

3 cups semisweet chocolate chips
1 14-ounce can sweetened
   condensed milk
Pinch salt

¾ cup chopped nuts, walnuts or
   pecans, optional
1½ teaspoons vanilla extract

Line an 8-inch square pan with waxed paper. Leave enough overhang to lift the fudge out when cooled.

In a heavy saucepan, heat the chocolate chips, condensed milk and salt over low heat. Stir occasionally until the chocolate chips have melted and mixture is smooth.

Remove from heat and cool slightly. Stir in vanilla. Add nuts, if using. Pour mixture into prepared pan and chill for 2 hours, or until firm.

Lift fudge out of pan, peel off wax paper and cut into squares. Store fudge in refrigerator.

Makes 25 pieces

Dried Schnitz Pie

Glick's Salads closed several years ago, but we wanted to keep this pie in the new edition of *The Reading Terminal Market Cookbook*. Michelle Fetter, who gave us this recipe, told us that dried apples have a concentrated flavor, and, like all dried fruits, they need to be reconstituted before being used in any dish.

3 cups sliced dried apple pieces	½ teaspoon ground cloves
1½ cups water	½ teaspoon cinnamon
⅓ cup sugar	
¼ cup molasses	Two 9-inch pie crusts

Preheat oven to 350 degrees.

Place dried apple pieces in a medium saucepan. Add the water, cover and simmer until soft, about 10 minutes. Drain in a colander, pressing apples gently to remove as much water as possible.

Add sugar, molasses, cloves and cinnamon to the apples. Place one pie crust in a 9-inch pie plate. Add the apple mixture and cover with the second pie crust. Press edges to seal. Use fork to poke several holes in the top pastry, and bake for 30 to 35 minutes, until top crust is nicely browned.

Serve warm or hot.

Makes six servings

Miller's Twist Soft Pretzels

Miller's Twist is famous for their regular pretzels and "Pretzel Roll-ups," which are stuffed with anything from eggs to rib eye steak and cheese. You can have fun twisting your own pretzels, or you can come to the Market and watch the Amish hand-roll the dough and enjoy a fresh and hot soft pretzel without the work.

5 cups water	½ cup brown sugar
1 tablespoon direct instant yeast	½ cup baking soda
6 cups all-purpose flour	Pretzel salt (coarse salt)
2 cups bread flour	¼ pound (1 stick) butter
1 teaspoon salt	

Heat 3 cups of the water until warm. Pour warm water into a large mixing bowl, sprinkle in 1 tablespoon of yeast and allow to rest for 1 minute. Add the all-purpose flour, bread flour, salt and brown sugar. Mix together until smooth (it should be a little sticky, but not too sticky to handle). Cover and let rise on a warm surface for 45 minutes. Heat the remaining 2 cups water to hot, add baking powder and stir until it dissolves. Set aside.

Preheat oven to 500 degrees.

Cut the dough with a pizza cutter into long strips. Roll into pieces 2½ to 3 feet long and shape into a pretzel. Dip the pretzels into the baking soda water and lay them on a baking sheet covered with parchment paper. Sprinkle coarse salt on the pretzels and put in oven. Bake for about 5 to 10 minutes, or until golden brown. Remove from oven and brush with melted butter.

Makes 16 to 18 pretzels

Old-Fashioned Apple Dumplings

Apple dumplings are a popular Pennsylvania Dutch specialty and a favorite at the Dutch Eating Place in the Market. Here is one version of this dish that we hope you'll enjoy. Make it in the fall, when apples are in their prime. Also, you can use a variety of apples, if desired.

2 cups brown sugar
2 cups water
¼ teaspoon cinnamon
¼ pound (1 stick) butter
2 cups flour
2½ teaspoons baking powder

½ teaspoon salt
⅔ cup shortening
½ cup whole milk
6 medium Rome apples, pared and
    cored but left whole
Hot milk or cream, optional

Preheat oven to 350 degrees.

Grease a jellyroll pan.

In a saucepan, combine brown sugar, water and cinnamon. Cook for 5 minutes, and then add the butter. Set aside.

In a bowl, sift together the flour, baking powder and salt. Cut in the shortening. Gradually pour in the milk, and mix lightly until the dough just holds together. Roll out dough and cut into six squares, each large enough to fully envelop the apple. Place an apple on each square, and fill the cavity of each apple with some of the brown sugar sauce. Pat dough around the apple to cover completely, making sure the dough is sealed on top.

Place dumplings 1 inch apart on the prepared pan. Pour any remaining sauce over the dumplings and bake for 45 to 50 minutes, or until the pastry is lightly golden. Serve in a bowl with hot milk or cream, if desired.

Makes six servings

Pennsylvania Dutch Funnel Cake

Funnel cake is so much fun to make and eat—a special treat for kids of all ages. A funnel cake pitcher or a regular funnel can be used to make these fried pastries. This is an easy version of a timeless treat.

1⅓ cups all-purpose flour
3 to 4 tablespoons sugar (or half cane and Demerara sugar)
1 teaspoon baking soda
⅛ teaspoon of salt
1 egg

1 cup whole milk (more if needed)
⅛ teaspoon pure vanilla extract, optional
Vegetable oil for frying
Confectioners' sugar for dusting

In a bowl, combine flour, sugar, baking soda and salt.

In another bowl, beat egg with milk and add vanilla, if using.

Combine wet and dry ingredients and stir until smooth. If batter is too thick, add a drop or two more of milk (it should have the consistency of pancake batter).

In a 10-inch skillet, heat oil, 1 inch deep, until hot but not smoking. Spoon about ½ cup of batter into a funnel (funnel opening should be no smaller than half an inch wide). Place a finger over funnel opening so batter won't drop out. Hold funnel over hot oil, release your finger and let batter stream slowly out of funnel. Use a circular motion, starting in center and working outward to form a spiral. Cook until lightly golden on one side, then using two spatulas, carefully turn over and cook other side. Funnel cakes will be done in about a minute. With a slotted spatula, remove from oil, allowing excess to drip off and place on paper towels to drain. (Place in a warm oven until remaining funnel cakes are cooked). Repeat with remaining batter.

Dust funnel cakes generously with confectioners' sugar and serve immediately.

Makes six funnel cakes

Roast Muscovy Duck with Sauerkraut and Herbs

This Pennsylvania Dutch recipe comes from L. Halteman Family Country Foods and has been a family favorite for generations. Sauerkraut complements the richness of the duck and is often paired with game dishes. Wild duck can also be prepared this way.

1 Muscovy duck, 4 to 5 pounds
1 teaspoon dried oregano
1 teaspoon dried marjoram

1 teaspoon dried sage
2 pounds sauerkraut, drained and
   rinsed

Preheat oven to 350 degrees.

Thoroughly rinse duck, inside and out, and pat dry. Remove excess fat from cavity. Season duck with oregano, marjoram and sage. Stuff duck with as much of the sauerkraut as will comfortably fill the cavity. Tie the legs together with string.

Add any remaining sauerkraut to bottom of roasting pan, and place duck on top. Cover and roast approximately 2½ hours. To test for doneness, wiggle the legs back and forth; if they move easily, the duck is fully cooked.

Remove duck from oven. Let stand for a few minutes, then carve into slices and serve with sauerkraut.

Makes four servings

Shoofly Pie

Beiler's Bakery gave us this well-known Pennsylvania Dutch recipe. Its main ingredient is molasses, once known as "the poor man's sugar." Legend has it that the sweetness of the pie attracted flies, which then had to be "shooed" away. Many Amish enjoy this pie at breakfast.

One 9-inch pie crust, homemade or
    store-bought
1 teaspoon baking soda
1 cup warm water
1 egg beaten

1 cup molasses
1½ cups flour
½ cup brown sugar
½ cup shortening

Preheat oven to 425 degrees.

Line a 9-inch pie plate with pastry crust.

In a medium bowl, dissolve the baking soda in the water. Mix in egg and molasses.

Place flour, sugar and shortening in another bowl and mix until crumbly. Mix ½ cup of the crumb mixture into the molasses mixture. Stir and pour into the prepared pie shell. Sprinkle the remaining crumbs evenly on top.

Bake for 15 minutes. Reduce heat to 350 degrees and bake for 30 minutes more, or until the center of the pie is firm.

Makes six servings

Sour Cherry Pie

This pie is juicy and delicious, especially when local sour cherries are in season. These cherries are quite tart, but they mellow during cooking. You can also prepare this pie using regular cherries. You will often find sour cherries at L. Halteman Family Country Foods.

1 8-inch pie crust

4 cups sour cherries
1 tablespoon flour
2 tablespoons quick-cooking tapioca
½ cup sugar

CRUMB TOPPING
5 ounces walnuts, finely chopped
½ cup sugar
4 tablespoons butter, softened
1 tablespoon flour
2 eggs, lightly beaten

Preheat oven to 350 degrees.

Line an 8-inch pie plate with the pastry. Refrigerate until ready to use.

Pit cherries over a bowl, where their juices can collect. To the juices, add flour, tapioca, sugar and cherries. Stir and let sit for about 10 minutes, until the flour and tapioca have been absorbed.

To make crumb topping, in a medium bowl, combine the walnuts, sugar, butter, flour and the eggs. Mix until blended. The mixture will be slightly sticky. Set aside.

Remove pie crust from refrigerator. Pour the cherry mixture into the crust and sprinkle crumb topping over cherries. Bake for about 45 minutes, or until the crust is lightly browned. Let cool and serve.

Makes six servings

Produce
Merchants

RECENT YEARS HAVE seen a heightened interest in vegetables, marked by an improvement in quality and an increased variety of local and imported produce. At the Market, you will find fresh cranberry beans, haricot verts, slender French beans, broccoli rabe, daikon and many different cabbages, including bok choy and savoy. In the summer, look for mounds of local corn and tomatoes, juicy peaches, apricots and nectarines—all mingling with strawberries, blueberries and raspberries.

Fair Food Farmstand opened in the Market in 2009. Since 2003, it has operated as the farm-to-consumer wing of Fair Food, a nonprofit organization dedicated to bringing local foods to the marketplace and promoting a humane, sustainable agricultural system in the Delaware Valley region. All products sold at the Farmstand—seasonal, sustainable produce; heritage-bred meats; grass-fed raw milk and dairy products, including artisan cheeses; and baked goods and value-added products like jams, honey and pickles—are sourced from family farms and food producers within a 150-mile radius of Philadelphia. Market customers can locate hard-to-find items like fiddlehead ferns and ramps in the spring, sour cherries and fresh figs in the summer, no-spray cranberries and heritage turkeys in the fall, and fresh, greenhouse-grown local produce in the winter—plus eggs, dairy, meats and pantry items year round. The Fair Food Farmstand harks back to the Market's initial purpose: a place for local growers to bring their goods to city customers. It combines the freshness of a traditional farmer's market with the convenience of a grocery store.

Over 15 years ago, Jimmy and Vinnie Iovine found a home for their business within the walls of Philadelphia's historic Reading Terminal Market. Since then, Iovine Brothers Produce has steadily grown into one of the city's most beloved grocers and a bona fide neighborhood staple. From the very beginning, the brothers knew that the key to lasting success would be hard work and unwavering loyalty to their customers. A commitment to these founding principles is what led Iovine Brothers Produce to achieve the success that it enjoys today. Their main desire is to provide the community with fresh products that will nourish and satisfy the soul. They are passionate about sharing their knowledge and their produce not only with the city they call home, but with the entire nation. There are mounds of vegetables and fruits displayed in abundance, ranging from the familiar to the very unusual. Iovine also carries yucca, plantains, red Cuban bananas, jicama and calabaza, among other specialties, and an extensive collection of fresh and dried mushrooms.

O.K. Lee Produce has been in the Market for several years and is currently owned by Yeoung O. Park. Their fruits and vegetables are artistically displayed throughout the stand. In addition to fresh produce, they carry fresh herbs, dried fruits and nuts. In addition, customers will find large selections of basic fruits and vegetables as well as some hard-to-locate items such as fresh sugar cane, cactus pears and fresh aloe. Local in-season produce is a popular seller, as are O.K. Lee's 99-cent grab bags full of tomatoes, red peppers, peaches and more.

All-Blue Mashed Potatoes

Fair Food Farmstand is an ideal local source for all-blue potatoes, which are more likely to be found in Peruvian markets. Their rich, bluish-purple color comes from the presence of anthocyanin, a compound noted for its strong antioxidants, making blue potatoes the most nutrient-rich of all varieties. This recipe will create mashed potatoes whose beautiful violet color is accompanied by a savory flavor.

6 pounds all-blue potatoes (Paridiese Organics), skin on, cut into small pieces

1½ pounds celeriac (celery root), peeled and cut into pieces

4 tablespoons butter, more if needed

2 small onions, chopped

1 to 2 garlic cloves, minced

Milk

Salt and pepper

4 scallions, finely chopped

In a large pan, bring water to a boil. Add potatoes and celeriac and cook about 10 minutes, or until tender. Drain potatoes and celeriac.

In a skillet, melt 2 tablespoons of the butter, add onions, and sauté until soft and translucent. Add minced garlic and place in a bowl.

Add all of the cooked celeriac and half of the potatoes to the onion and garlic mixture, then stir and mash to combine. Add enough milk and the remaining two tablespoons of butter (more if needed) to moisten the potatoes. Using an immersion blender, puree until smooth.

Coarsely mash the remaining potatoes and add to the pureed mixture. Mix well. Add salt and pepper to taste.

Mix in the finely chopped scallions and serve.

Makes four to six servings

Baked Fennel

Fennel is delicious eaten raw in a salad or dipped in olive oil. Slow cooking brings out its characteristic sweet anise flavor that goes so well with roasts and game dishes. Fennel can be found at any of the produce stands in the Market.

4 fennel bulbs, sliced in half, each half cut into thin slices
1 cup chopped fresh basil, or 1 tablespoon dried
5 tablespoons extra virgin olive oil

Preheat oven to 350 degrees.

Place fennel slices on a baking sheet, sprinkle with basil and drizzle with olive oil. Toss lightly to coat fennel.

Bake, covered, for 15 minutes. Uncover and cook and additional 15 minutes, or until fennel is tender. Serve hot or at room temperature.

Makes four servings

Fennel is available at all of the produce stands at the Market.

Balsamic Glazed Herbed Mushrooms

This flavorful mushroom recipe comes from Fair Food Farmstand. Fair Food carries a large selection of mushrooms, including shiitake, cremini, oyster and portobello. Any of these mushroom varieties would work well in this recipe.

2 tablespoons olive oil

2 tablespoons unsalted butter

1 pound cremini mushrooms,
  cleaned and halved

2 tablespoons dry vermouth or
  white wine

2 tablespoons balsamic vinegar

1 teaspoon chopped rosemary

1 teaspoon chopped thyme

Salt and pepper to taste

In a sauté pan, combine the olive oil and butter over medium heat. Add mushrooms and sauté until tender, about 7 to 8 minutes.

Add vermouth or wine and cook until liquid has been absorbed, about 1 minute. Add balsamic vinegar and reduce until the mushrooms are glazed. Add fresh rosemary, thyme, salt and pepper, and toss.

Makes four servings

The produce display at Fair Food Farmstand.

Honey and Spiced Pears

This delicious pear recipe is great to make all year round, but especially in the fall and winter. Iovine Brothers Produce supplied us with this recipe. Their stand is a good place to find dried cranberries and other dried fruits.

1 cup cranberry juice
¾ teaspoon ground cinnamon
¼ teaspoon ground allspice

4 small, firm pears, peeled, halved
   and cored
2 tablespoons dried cranberries
1 tablespoon honey

In a large nonstick skillet, combine cranberry juice, cinnamon and allspice. Add pears and cranberries. Bring to a boil over medium-high heat. Cover and cook for 5 minutes, or until pears are just tender-crisp. Transfer pears cut side down to a serving plate. Leave the liquid in the skillet. Stirring frequently, cook liquid for 2 to 3 minutes, or until reduced to a scant ¼ cup. Remove from heat. Stir in honey, spoon over the pears and allow to cool completely before serving.

Makes four servings

Irina Smith's Curried Carrot Soup

My mother made wonderful soups, especially during the cold, rainy English winter months. This is a variation of a soup she used to make. It's good either in winter or summer, hot or cold. Adapt the coriander and curry powder more or less according to your taste. Sometimes I add plain yogurt instead of coconut milk. This soup freezes well.

2 tablespoons unsalted butter
2 tablespoons vegetable oil
2 pounds carrots, peeled and thinly
    sliced
1 large onion, chopped
2 leeks, cleaned and sliced
4 garlic cloves, chopped
2 tablespoons fresh ginger, chopped
1 teaspoon seeded and minced fresh
    serrano or jalapeño pepper

1 tablespoon ground coriander
1 tablespoon curry powder
Sea salt
Freshly ground black pepper
8 cups chicken stock
¾ cup coconut milk
2 tablespoons lime juice
Fresh cilantro leaves for garnish

Heat butter and oil in a large saucepan over medium heat. Add carrots, onions and leeks. Cook, stirring occasionally, until slightly softened, about 15 minutes. Add garlic, ginger, peppers, coriander, curry powder, and a generous pinch of sea salt and black pepper. Cook for another 2 to 3 minutes. Pour in the chicken stock, cover partially, and bring to a boil. Reduce heat and simmer gently until the vegetables are very soft, about 20 to 25 minutes.

Remove from heat and cool.

In either a food processor or blender, puree the soup in batches to desired consistency. Pour into a large bowl, then add the coconut milk and lime juice. Chill if serving cold. Heat through if serving hot. Garnish with cilantro leaves.

Makes four to six servings

Jimmy Iovine's Kickin' Kale Chips

This is a guilt-free, you-just-can't-stop-at-one-bite snack. Perfect for nights at home in front of the TV as well as entertaining. "Who doesn't love to eat kale chips?" says Jimmy Iovine of Iovine Brothers Produce. (That's certainly true for everyone who has tried them before.) Add other seasonings, if desired.

1 bunch kale
1 tablespoon olive oil

1 teaspoon seasoned salt

Preheat oven to 350 degrees.

Line a cookie sheet with parchment paper.

With a knife or kitchen shears, carefully remove the leaves from the thick stems of the kale, and tear into bite-size pieces.

Wash and thoroughly dry kale with a salad spinner. Drizzle it with olive oil and sprinkle with seasoned salt. Place pieces on the cookie sheet and bake until their edges are brown but are not burnt, about 10 to 15 minutes. Serve immediately.

Makes four servings

Market Customer: Dorothy Ann Hazan

D.A. has loved the Market since the days when I would spend hours there running errands and researching the first *Reading Terminal Market Cookbook*. I'd push her along in a stroller past Bassetts Ice Cream and Famous 4th Street Cookies. There were other vendors around, but she distinctly remembers Bassetts Ice Cream and Famous 4th Street Cookies. These days, D.A. frequents the Market voluntarily. She has a flare for unique and creative ways of preparing food.

Eggplant-Tomato Salsa

This recipe for eggplant-tomato salsa is D.A.'s creation. It pairs well with chicken, lamb, pork, beef, fish and rice, making it the ideal side dish.

1 medium eggplant	1 teaspoon red wine vinegar
4 tablespoons olive oil	¼ teaspoon chili powder
1 garlic clove, minced	¼ teaspoon sweet paprika
1 cup chopped onion	⅛ teaspoon red chili flakes
½ cup chopped green bell pepper	Salt and pepper to taste
½ cup chopped tomatoes	Sriracha chili-garlic sauce to taste

Peel the eggplant and slice into ½-inch-thick rounds. Lay rounds on paper towels and sprinkle salt over eggplant on both sides. After 20 minutes, beads of liquid will form on the surface. Rinse eggplant and gently squeeze out liquid. This will make it less bitter. Chop eggplant into ½-inch cubes and set aside.

Heat 1 tablespoon of the olive oil in a skillet and add garlic and onion. Cook until fragrant, about 2 to 3 minutes. Put mixture in a large bowl. Add remaining 3 tablespoons of olive oil to skillet and sauté eggplant for about 15 minutes, or until lightly browned. Remove from heat.

Add chopped peppers to the bowl containing the onions, garlic and oil. Next, add chopped tomatoes. Then add eggplant and toss mixture to combine.

Add red wine vinegar, chili powder, paprika, chili flakes, salt, pepper and Sriracha sauce. Toss to incorporate spices. Serve.

Makes four to six servings

An assortment of Market vegetables to be used in making eggplant-tomato salsa.

Market Customer: Ellen Steiner

Ellen works in real estate in Philadelphia, and has been shopping at the Reading Terminal Market for many years. She finds that buying the freshest ingredients is essential to her cooking. Ellen has prepared this dish many times and says it's great for parties.

Potatoes au Gratin

1 pound new potatoes, skin on, scrubbed
1 teaspoon salt

½ teaspoon freshly ground black pepper
2 cups heavy cream
1 garlic clove, cut in half

Cut potatoes into ⅓-inch-thick slices and place in a large saucepan. Season with salt and pepper.

In another saucepan, bring cream to a boil and pour over potatoes. Cook covered over very low heat, stirring occasionally for 1½ to 2 hours until most of the cream is absorbed and thickened. Add more hot cream if necessary.

Meanwhile, rub a gratin dish with the cut garlic.

Preheat broiler.

When potatoes are cooked, spoon them into the gratin dish. Place under the broiler for 1 to 2 minutes, or until the potatoes are lightly browned.

Makes four to six servings

Market Customer: Fabian Cortez

Fabian Cortez, a native Philadelphian, comes to the Market not only to see his cousin, Michael Holahan, who owns the Pennsylvania General Store, but also to shop. Fabian enjoys cooking and gave us this recipe, which he says was passed on to him by a good friend.

Savoy Cabbage and Beans

Olive oil

4 ounces fatback or pancetta, diced

2 garlic cloves, chopped

2 heads Savoy cabbage, sliced

½ cup water

2 19-ounce cans white kidney beans

Salt and freshly ground black
   pepper to taste

1 teaspoon crushed red pepper
   flakes

Cover the bottom of a large, heavy saucepan with oil. Add fatback or pancetta and brown over medium heat until crisp. Do not drain. Add garlic and sauté for about 1 minute. Then add cabbage and water. Stir and cover. Cook until cabbage is tender, about 15 minutes. Do not overcook. Add beans with their liquid, stir, and season with salt and pepper. Then add crushed red pepper and simmer until beans have heated through.

Makes four to six servings

Panzanella

This recipe uses heirloom tomatoes, which when available, can be found at the produce stands in the Market, or you can grow your own from seeds purchased at Market Blooms. Other varieties of tomatoes may be used, in addition to vegetables such as bell peppers and onions. The cheese can also be varied with the many selections available at the cheese shops in the Market.

¼ cup extra virgin olive oil
1 to 2 tablespoons red wine vinegar
4 heirloom tomatoes, chopped
   (other varieties may be used)
1 small seedless cucumber, chopped
¼ cup ricotta salata cheese, cubed

¼ cup basil leaves, chopped
½ cup croutons (see Homemade
   croutons below)
Salt and freshly ground pepper to
   taste

In a small bowl, whisk together oil and vinegar.

In another bowl, combine tomatoes, cucumber, cheese, basil leaves and croutons. Season with salt and pepper to taste. Add oil mixture, toss and serve.

Makes four servings

———

Homemade croutons: To make, cut slices of bread (preferably Italian or French bread), then cut into cubes. Heat a little oil in a skillet, add bread cubes and a pinch of salt, and cook over medium heat, tossing frequently for about 5 minutes, or until lightly browned. Croutons can also be made in the oven at 350 degrees for about 20 minutes. Toss lightly with oil before cooking.

Rosemary Vegetable Skewers

This is a great summer grilling dish from Jimmy and Vinnie of Iovine Brothers Produce. The recipe is very flexible. If you prefer using crimini mushrooms, go right ahead. Have a craving for broccoli or cauliflower? Throw them on—the possibilities are endless. Keep the rosemary needles you remove from the sprigs, dry them and save for later use.

4 fresh rosemary sprigs	8 medium button mushrooms,
1 tablespoon fresh rosemary,	cleaned, stems removed
minced	4 grape tomatoes
4 tablespoon olive oil	4 1-inch pieces yellow bell pepper
Salt and pepper to taste	

Preheat grill or grill pan.

Remove three-quarters of the rosemary needles from the sprigs, creating a skewer. Set the sprigs aside. Mince rosemary needles.

In a small bowl, whisk together olive oil, minced rosemary, and salt and pepper to taste.

To assemble the skewers, place a mushroom, a tomato, a pepper and another mushroom onto a rosemary skewer. Continue with the remaining vegetables and skewers.

Brush oil mixture over the vegetables. Place the skewers onto the hot grill or grill pan and cook for approximately 2 minutes per side. Serve and enjoy.

Makes four skewers

Stir-Fried Chinese Cabbage

Chinese cabbage, sometimes called bok choy, is a white-stalked, green-leafed cabbage with a slightly bitter taste. If cooked quickly, it retains its crispness and mellow flavor. This recipe comes from O.K. Lee Produce.

2 heads bok choy about 1½ pounds, washed thoroughly
3 tablespoons vegetable oil
1 1-inch slice of gingerroot, peeled and chopped

1 garlic clove, chopped
1 tablespoon water
1 tablespoon rice wine vinegar
Pinch salt
2 teaspoons sesame oil

Trim stem ends from bok choy, removing any tough pieces. Cut the leaves and stems into 1-inch slices and keep them separate.

Heat a wok or skillet over high heat. Add the oil, toss in the ginger and garlic, and stir-fry for about 5 seconds. Add sliced bok choy stems and toss for a few seconds. Add water, cover and cook about 1 minute. Add sliced bok choy leaves, vinegar and salt. Stir-fry for about 45 seconds, or until leaves have wilted. Drizzle with sesame oil. Serve hot or at room temperature.

Makes four servings

"Taller Than William Penn" Veggie and Hummus Tower

The "Taller Than William Penn" reference in the name of this recipe is based on the old Philadelphia rule that no building could be taller than the William Penn statue atop City Hall. Since the dish is a highly stacked tower of vegetables, it seems appropriately named by Jimmy and Vinnie, owners of Iovine Brothers Produce.

1 large red onion, peeled, trimmed and cut into 6 slices
2 large red bell peppers, cored and sliced into 3 pieces
2 large yellow bell peppers, cored and sliced into 3 pieces
1 large zucchini, halved and sliced lengthwise to make 6 pieces
1 large yellow squash, halved and sliced lengthwise to make 6 pieces
1 medium-large eggplant, trimmed and sliced into 6 pieces
6 large portobello mushroom caps, stemmed, with gills removed
½ cup olive oil
3 tablespoons balsamic vinegar

3 garlic cloves, chopped
1 teaspoon each of dried thyme, dill and parsley
Sea salt and ground pepper to taste

LEMON HUMMUS
1 14-ounce can chickpeas (garbanzo beans), with liquid reserved
Zest and juice of one large lemon
2 tablespoons sesame tahini or almond butter
1 garlic clove, peeled and crushed
Pinch sea salt
4 tablespoons extra virgin olive oil
Chives, optional

In a large bowl, combine onion, bell peppers, zucchini, yellow squash, eggplant and portobello mushrooms.

In a small bowl, thoroughly combine olive oil, balsamic vinegar, garlic, thyme, dill and parsley. Pour oil mixture over the vegetables, season with sea salt and ground pepper to taste. Gently toss, cover and marinate for 1 hour.

Heat grill to medium high.

Place the vegetables in a grill basket or on a large sheet of foil. Place on hot grill, cover and cook 15 to 20 minutes, or until the vegetables are tender-crisp. If necessary, cook in batches. Remove vegetables to a large platter and set aside.

While vegetables are cooking, make lemon hummus. Combine chickpeas, lemon juice, lemon zest, tahini, garlic and sea salt in a food processor. Pulse briefly to combine. With processor running, pour in olive oil and a little of the reserved chickpea liquid. Process until creamy. Place in a serving bowl. Cover and chill until needed.

To create a vegetable stack, place the portobello mushroom cap on a serving plate and layer it with a spoonful of lemon hummus. Add eggplant, peppers, zucchini and onion, spreading a little of the humus between each layer. Top with a dab of hummus. If desired, sprinkle with fresh chopped chives. Repeat for the remaining five servings.

Makes six servings

Fresh bell peppers on display at Iovine's Produce.

Vinnie Iovine's Chocolate Fruit Tacos

This delicious and tasty recipe from Vinnie of Iovine Brothers Produce is good on hot, sultry summer days. Agave nectar is an organic natural sweetener made from the extract of the blue agave. This sweetener is slightly less viscous than honey, which makes it easy to use in a variety dishes.

1 cup whole wheat flour
3 cups all-purpose flour
1 teaspoon baking powder
¼ teaspoon salt
⅓ cup cocoa powder
⅓ cup coconut oil
4 tablespoons agave nectar
1½ cups warm water

½ cup blueberries, washed
1 cup strawberries, chopped
2 kiwis, diced
1 mango, diced
½ cup diced pineapple, diced
Juice of 1 lime
Honey or fresh mint, optional

In a large bowl, whisk together whole wheat flour, all-purpose flour, baking powder, salt and cocoa.

Add coconut oil, agave nectar and warm water to the dry ingredients. Mix together with a wooden spoon until a large ball of dough forms. Transfer dough to a floured work surface and knead for five minutes, adding additional flour if the dough is too sticky to handle.

Divide the dough in half and roll both pieces into a ball. Continue to divide the dough until there are 16 pieces. Let dough rest for 10 minutes. Transfer one piece of dough to a floured work surface and roll into a circle that is one-quarter-inch thick and about five inches in diameter.

Heat a cast-iron skillet over medium heat. Do not add oil to skillet. Once the skillet is hot, add the rolled-out dough and cook for 30 seconds. Flip the dough and cook for an additional 30 seconds. Repeat until all of the 16 pieces of dough have been used. Transfer tortillas to a plate lined with a damp paper towel.

In a bowl, add blueberries, strawberries, kiwis, mango and pineapple, and drizzle with lime juice.

Glazed garlic lamb ribs from Border Spring Lamb Farm *(see page 53)*.

ABOVE: Baked fish
with tomatoes and
olives *(see page 82)*.

LEFT: Curried carrot
soup *(see page 117)*.

RIGHT: Bread pudding from Beck's Cajun Café *(see pages 143–144)*.

BELOW: The Train Wreck sandwich from Beck's Cajun Café *(see page 145)*.

ABOVE: Banana and Nutella crêpe from Profi's Crêperie *(see page 152)*.

Photo courtesy of Sarah Morrison, All About Events catering, Reading Terminal Market.

RIGHT: Michelle Leff's shrimp enchilada and guacamole plate from 12th Street Cantina *(see pages 158 and 163–164)*.

To serve, place chocolate tortilla on individual plates. Distribute fruit evenly among tortillas and top with honey or mint if desired. Roll tortillas enclosing the filling to form tacos.

Makes 16 tacos

Jimmy and Vinnie Iovine.

Wild Mushroom Casserole

This can be used as a stuffing for pork, chicken or veal, or it can be baked separately as a side dish. All the produce stands carry a variety of mushrooms. Thoroughly cleaning mushrooms is important; they absorb liquids like a sponge, so don't soak them in water. Instead, gently brush the dirt away with a damp paper towel. If they are full of sand, rinse quickly but make sure they are well-dried. Store mushrooms in a paper bag or ceramic container; kept in plastic, they will turn mushy. Morels are dark brown with a nutlike taste. Chanterelles are trumpet-shaped with a light, delicate flavor. Oyster mushrooms are beige with a mild flavor. Porcini and portobellos are large and brown with a meaty, smoky flavor. Shiitake are tawny with flat caps and a rich, nutty taste.

¼ pound (1 stick) butter
1½ pounds fresh wild mushrooms
 (such as morels, shiitakes,
 chanterelles, oysters, or
 portobellos), sliced
1 onion, diced
1 cup minced celery

2 cups bread cubes
1 tablespoon minced fresh sage
½ tablespoon minced fresh
 marjoram
1½ teaspoons salt
1 teaspoon pepper

Preheat oven to 325 degrees.

Grease a 2½-quart casserole.

Melt butter in a large skillet over low heat. Add mushrooms, onion and celery, and sauté for about 5 minutes. Remove from heat. Add bread cubes, sage, marjoram, salt and pepper, mixing to coat well. Let sit for a few minutes to absorb any juices.

Place mushroom mixture into prepared casserole and bake for 45 minutes to 1 hour.

Makes four servings

Restaurants

EOPLE FROM ALL walks of life make their way to the Reading Terminal Market each day to visit their favorite food stall or to have a new breakfast experience. Early shoppers arrive, heading to a particular meat, fish or vegetable stand to beat the crowds. By the lunch hour, the scene is bustling. The choices are endless for eating "Reading Terminal Market style." Making your way down the aisles, you will be struck by the sights, sounds and aromas of the Market—all of which illustrate how it is as great a place to sit down and have a meal as it is to find the ingredients to take home and make a meal.

At the white-tiled counter and sitting area of the 12th Street Cantina, you'll enjoy a whole line of contemporary and traditional Mexican dishes. After 30 years, owner Michelle Leff is still considered the Market's aficionada on all things Mexican. Michelle traveled in Mexico, exploring local cuisines and perfecting tortilla recipes. Her repertoire of Mexican foods has earned her a good reputation, and she has worked hard to find the ingredients that make her foods authentic. Display cases and shelves are filled with fresh and dried chilies, cactus plants and salsas of all varieties, jars of mole, beans and fresh tortillas. The many different dishes prepared here can be enjoyed for lunch or taken home for a wonderful taste of Mexico at dinnertime.

Beck's Cajun Café in the Market brings to Philadelphia the exotic and flavorful foods of New Orleans and southern Louisiana. Award-winning chef Bill Beck began his distinguished career in Philadelphia more than 25 years ago. In 2009, he returned to his roots by opening Beck's Cajun Café. Stop by for their Bourbon Street Breakfast, and when beignets are available, enjoy these French doughnuts served piping hot and topped with confectioners' sugar. Lunch and dinner menu items—including muffaletta sandwiches, jambalaya, gumbos, po' boys and bread pudding—seem like they've been airlifted directly from the cafés of the French Quarter. At Beck's, you can find original condiments and spice blends as well as rubs and seasonings for chicken, seafood and steaks under the Beck's Kitchen Pantry label, recently featured in the *Philadelphia Business Journal.* Take a quick trip to The Big Easy at Beck's.

At Mezze Mediterranean Foods, owned by Kim Mickel, the selections wrap around three sides of the stand, including one side with a make-your-own salad station. You can start your day with a breakfast sandwich on homemade focaccia, or stop by for lunch or dinner to sample one of their signature sandwiches on a seeded baguette. At the salad station, you can find Mezze's top seller, Santorini Greek salad, or put together a salad of your own.

George Mickel of By George Pizza, Pasta and Cheesesteaks.

By George Pizza, Pasta & Cheesesteaks is where you will find owner George Mickel busy baking fragrant and flavorful pizzas, strombolis and calzonis in his brick oven. As you walk past, glance at the cases filled with fresh and frozen ravioli, tortellini, gnocchi and homemade sauces—many of them great choices for a meal ready to take home. Take a minute to watch fresh pasta dough being cut into different widths and to look at the many prepared Italian specialties, from lasagna to simmering trays of sausage, peppers and onions. A panorama of multicolored bell peppers, sun-dried tomatoes, mounds of marinated fresh mozzarella and hot cherry peppers filled with provolone complete the picture.

Carmen's Famous Italian Hoagies & Cheesesteaks is owned and operated by Carmen DiGuglielmo and his wife, Tina. Their family-run business has been in the Market for the past 30 years. They have been featured in numerous papers, including *The Philadelphia Inquirer*. Carmen's has won Best of Philly several times, and awards for one of the best hoagies in the Market. They are widely known for their authentic Italian and specialty hoagies. But Philadelphia's best-known culinary invention—the cheesesteak—also ranks high as a "must try" for locals and tourists alike.

Tommy DiNic's is a popular sandwich counter that is owned by a father and son, Tommy and Joe Nicolosi. Each day, they both arrive early to supervise the cooking of their specialties: pulled pork, beef brisket, and roast pork and beef. Slow oven roasting produces meats that are succulent and juicy. Many Market merchants choose DiNic's as a place to relax and savor a hearty sandwich. DiNic's was featured on *Man v. Food* and several other TV shows, and it has been written about extensively in newspapers and national magazines. It has come in first among the 30 best sandwiches in America. Giving the Philly cheesesteak a run for its money is the famous DiNic's roast pork sandwich. Joe Nicolosi, the head chef, slices thin, juicy, slow-roasted pork; layers it on a freshly baked roll; and tops it with sharp provolone and broccoli rabe. A sprinkling more of gravy and you'll know why hungry customers must scoot quickly to get a seat at the counter. DiNic's is in a new, larger space now, with an added take-out section, but every additional seat is still taken during the lunch hour.

One might want to start with breakfast at Reading Terminal Market's Down Home Diner. Jack McDavid, one of Philadelphia's best-known restaurateurs and a man whose name is synonymous with "down-home cooking," is committed to maintaining the true ambiance of a diner as a Market attraction. Breakfast is popular here, with huge portions of cheese grits or ham with red-eye gravy and biscuits that bring back memories of hearty, old-fashioned, early-day meals. From mid-morning on, customers wait patiently for a table to enjoy the hospitality and comfort foods that McDavid offers. The diner now has a separate counter where dishes are available for take-out. Many of the lunch and dinner choices are good reflections of the ambiance: pecan-crusted catfish platter, catfish po'boy sandwich, fried chicken with collard greens, pulled pork hoagie, barbecued ribs; hearty soups like black-eyed pea with ham and potato with ham and leeks; and good old mac 'n cheese.

Then there's America's favorite sausage—the hot dog. At Franks A-Lot, owner Russell Black has been widely recognized for his success with that once-humble food. His secret is to serve lean and tasty dogs. Unusual toppings accompany these traditional franks. His pizza-and-hoagie dog and the traditional Texas Tommy and chili dog have been acclaimed by many lunch customers as the Market's best. Russell has also perfected the french fry. His are somewhat different, a cross between a potato chip and a regular french fry. We once caught one of the Market's meat merchants sitting at the counter, enjoying a plateful of these addictive fries. "The best in town," she said.

Respect for good food is an integral part of the Chinese way of life. There are five main regional styles of cooking in China, and Golden Bowl gives the Market the flavors and tastes of Mandarin, Szechuan and Hunan-style cooking. Pan Kai Maw and her husband, Michael, opened the stand in 1983, and their son, David, did most of the preparation and cooking. In 1997, Ms. Maw passed on her recipes to the current owner, Soon Ae Mun, of Korean heritage. He has added an American-Asian fusion style to the recipes. But loyal customers can be assured that the sauces used in the dishes are as wonderful as ever.

Hershel's East Side Deli serves up classic hand-carved deli sandwiches and authentic homemade Jewish specialties. Steven Safern, whose uncle was a partner at Katz's in New York, has truly brought us the New York deli experience: matzo ball soup, chopped chicken liver, whitefish salad, potato latkes with sour cream or applesauce, knishes, sandwiches stacked high with corned beef, pastrami or brisket and crowned with Russian dressing and coleslaw, and all-beef hot dogs with sauerkraut. No deli would be complete without an assortment of Dr. Brown's soda and New York egg creams. For the grand finale, the deli features Jewish apple cake and New York cheesecake.

Kamal's Middle Eastern Specialties—run by Kamal Albarouki and his wife, Rose, along with their children, Hesham, Hanna, Anwar and Adham—demon-

Kamal and Rose Albarouki, proprietors of Kamal's Middle Eastern Specialties.

strates the true meaning of family-operated. Kamal and Rose arrived in the United States in the mid-1970s and ran a small grocery in South Philadelphia. In 1983, they opened Kamal's Middle Eastern Specialties in the Market. You'll often see them behind the counter, busily preparing a myriad of Middle Eastern favorites, including falafel, shawerma, lamb dishes and spicy Moroccan chicken. They have homemade spinach pie, hummus and tabbouleh, as well as an assortment of pastries including kataifi and traditional baklava. There is also a counter offering a variety of freshly made juices.

Thai food, fresh Asian herbs and groceries can be found at the Little Thai Market, owned by Tak and Kaysone Lam. Little Thai has been a part of the Market for more than 10 years. The shelves are lined with lime leaves, lemongrass, bamboo shoots, chili-garlic sauce, red curry paste, tom yum paste and coconut milk—just about everything you'll need to prepare a great Thai meal at home. Already prepared foods to eat in or take out include salmon curry, Thai barbecued chicken, spicy shrimp, traditional pad Thai, yellow and red curry, and soups made with coconut and lemongrass. We were told that the sauce accompanying the popular salmon curry is so delicious that customers always request a little extra.

After naming Iovine Brothers Produce after their father, owners Jimmy and Vinnie Iovine decided to honor the memory of their mother by naming their new business venture Molly Malloy's. They expanded and purchased what was once known as The Beer Garden. After extensive renovations and discovering Philadelphia's best-kept secret—chef Bobby Fisher—they are proud to have opened the Market's first "gastropub," focusing on preparing innovative dishes using the freshest produce available. Molly Malloy's is the only restaurant in the Market serving alcoholic beverages. You can enjoy handcrafted selections from their extensive menu with a drink from their full-service bar or a glass or two of beer from over 24 choices on tap.

Nanee's Kitchen is an Indian-Pakistani food stand and grocery that was started by two sisters, Tayyaba Khanum and Khalida Ahmad. They use recipes handed down by their mother, for whom the store is named. The aroma of exquisitely spiced Indian food, made fresh daily, soon drew customers their way. Khalida's son, Da'nish, and his wife, Sabina, joined the business and now manage the newly expanded location. Nanee's Kitchen specializes in gluten-free, vegan and vegetarian dishes. In addition, they have tandoori (clay oven) dishes using lamb, chicken, beef and salmon. A perfectly seasoned chicken korma is among their most popular items, along with their tasty baked samosas. Nanee's also serves homemade lassi—yogurt drinks made from mango, cardamom, rose water and pomegranate.

Molly Malloy's, owned by Jimmy and Vinnie Iovine, is the Market's first gastropub.

Athens and Roula Voulgaridis, proprietors of Olympia Gyro,
providing Greek and Mediterranean specialties.

Olympia Gyro is owned and operated by Athens and Roula Voulgaridis, who took over the family business from Athens' father George a few years ago. For years, Olympia Gyro was named Olympic Gyro. It had to be changed after the United States Olympic Committee informed them of their copyright. George Voulgaridis had worked in many restaurants while in Thessaloniki, Greece. After coming to America, he continued to work in restaurants in Philadelphia. When George, along with his wife, Despina, came across the Reading Terminal Market, they fell in love with it and had the opportunity to become merchants there in 1984. Athens and Roula insist on providing their customers with traditional taste, but with a modern-day twist. They also do catering that specializes in Mediterranean cuisine.

Kevin Parker's Soul Food Café is located where another Southern soul food purveyor, Delilah's at the Terminal, once was. The décor is top-notch and the seating is cozy and a bit removed from the maddening crowd. Kevin's specialties include crispy fried chicken, macaroni and cheese, salads, fried catfish, yams, greens, desserts and the not-to-be-missed chicken and waffles. Kevin is also the owner of another soul food restaurant, Ms. Tootsie's, on South Street.

Today's patrons of Pearl's Oyster Bar may not know its history and that it originally occupied a far larger portion of Reading Terminal Market. Fresh fish was brought in daily and was displayed on one side of the aisle and beyond, along with lunch counters where customers would sit and consume large platters of fried fish and oysters. It was once owned by one of the longtime merchant families in the Market, the Margerums. They sold the fish part of their business in the early 1930s to Vincent Cardello, and it became Vincent's Seafood. At one time, live turtles were brought in to prepare snapper soup from scratch. In the late '40s, he sold to a woman who gave the business her own name, calling it Pearl's Oyster Bar. Pearl installed the Market's first lobster tanks, which remained until she sold to "Iggy" Reynolds. In the early 1970s, Reynolds remodeled the portion along the 12th Street side. He kept the name, and today, Pearl's Oyster Bar is as popular a spot in the Market as it ever was. Pearl's present owners, Lisa and Dani Braunstein, have continued serving the traditional seafood platters, prepared by their wonderful, cheerful cook. Every day, customers lunching at the black-and-white tiled counter enjoy Pearl's longstanding tradition of serving large platters of fried or broiled fish, fried oysters and clams, crab cakes, oysters and clams on the half shell, big bowls of oyster stew and snapper soup, and countless other outstanding seafood dishes and sandwiches. Pearl's Oyster Bar now serves breakfast. The breakfast menu includes such selections as smoked salmon Benedict, shrimp and grits as well as standard breakfast items.

No trip to Paris needed. Profi's Crêperie, owned by George Profi, has been in the Market for 10 years. Here you can experience exceptional crêpes at their best— white or whole wheat, savory or sweet, and made to order. Enjoy a warm crêpe filled with bacon, egg and cheese; chicken with fresh vegetables and goat cheese or with tomato and pesto; with Nutella, banana and strawberries; apple, walnut and honey; or choose your own filling combinations. The best part is sitting at the counter and watching them being made, poured, flipped, filled, folded and brought right to you.

Sang Kee Peking Duck, owned by Michael and Jie Chow, has offered outstanding food for more than 30 years. Their succulently prepared duck is served in many different ways, often with rice or noodles, or in soups. According to Jie Chow, in addition to their famous Peking duck platters, the duck wonton noodle soup and the wonton vegetable soup are among Sang Kee's most popular menu items. They also serve incredible steamed and pan-fried dumplings, baby bok choy, Hong Kong roast pork and a variety of lo mein and fried rice dishes.

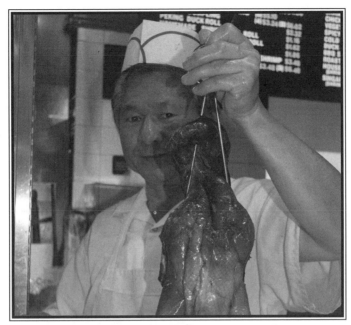

The specialty at Sang Kee Peking Duck.

Shanghai Gourmet Restaurant is owned by Stephen Shao and is a great destination for those in search of Hunan, Mandarin and Szechuan platters and soups. Their most popular dish is General Tso's chicken, which will have you coming back for more. Other favorites include Mongolian beef, sesame or orange chicken, shrimp and broccoli, and excellently prepared tofu with black bean or curry sauce. Many customers prefer brown rice as an alternative to white. Shanghai Gourmet is always crowded, and for the best reason—its food is always good.

Spataro's Cheesesteaks features hoagies, cheesesteaks, lunch and breakfast sandwiches, and the cream cheese and olive original that appeared on their menu when the shop first opened in the Market. Best-sellers at the stand are the Italian hoagie, the classic Philly cheesesteak and the corned beef special. Domenic C. Spataro started his career during the 1930s by working after school at Troelsch, one of three buttermilk stands in the Market. It was the forerunner of today's health food shops. In addition to buttermilk, it sold whole wheat muffins and raw vegetable sandwiches. After his military service, Dom worked at the Market for the Stevens family; there he met his wife. In 1947, the family sold the business to him, and Spataro's was born. In an interview with Dom in 1997, he remembered the horses and carts, which were used for pickups and deliveries around the city. He recalled the 1940s, when Philadelphians holding ration coupons waited in long lines to buy milk and butter at what was practically the only place in the city selling these items. Dressed poultry—some hanging with feathers still visible—and sides of meat swinging from hooks were all around the Market. The original Spataro's stand sold buttermilk. A sign above their business read, "Drink Buttermilk, Live Forever." The sign remains at the original location, now occupied by Terralyn Soaps. Customers back then would stop by for a sandwich with buttermilk. The sandwiches cost only 10 cents (13 cents for ham and cheese, among the most popular). Root beer from the barrel was a favorite beverage. Renamed Spataro's Cheesesteaks, the business is currently owned by Domenic Mark Spataro, son of the original owner, and now occupies an expanded stand in the Market. It's as busy as ever, and Domenic along with his son, Alex, a food science major in college, are still keeping their longtime family tradition alive.

Since 1983, the Market has enjoyed the aroma of freshly roasting turkeys at The Original Turkey. Roger Bassett started the business by offering just one sandwich—turkey, lettuce and tomato. It became so popular that he branched out and created a whole turkey theme. "All we do is turkey," said Roger as we watched thick, juicy, hand-carved slices being served on freshly baked bread and turkey soup being ladled out. The menu now includes a turkey "steak" sandwich; a Texas griller with provolone and petal sauce (similar to horseradish); a Florentine wrap with spinach, swiss cheese and pepper-Parmesan sauce; a western quesadilla with pepper jack cheese and chipotle sauce, all topped with roasted peppers and onions. Customers still line up for their freshly roasted turkey sandwiches and platters, served with mashed potatoes and gravy, macaroni and cheese, collard greens and corn.

Tootsie's Salad Express is owned by Tootsie Iovine. At the same location for decades, it began as Salad Express under two different ownerships. Tootsie, who had worked there for 20 years, purchased the business about eight years ago. Customers flock there for the extensive salad bar, the freshest anywhere. They have a variety of lettuces and other greens and numerous toppings, including grilled chicken, grilled tuna and ham. Each day, a selection of hot and cold buffet-style foods, as well as a special of the day, is served. The choices may include fried whiting, rosemary chicken, fried chicken, chicken marsala, or traditional meatloaf. Among the side dishes are collard greens, sweet potatoes and mac 'n cheese. Tootsie's does lots of take-out business, but some customers like to sit at the counter and take in all the wafting aromas.

A welcome addition to the Market is Wursthaus Schmitz with its homemade German specialties. Wursthaus Schmitz, a spin-off of the venerable South Street beer hall and restaurant, Brauhaus Schmitz, is a German delikatessen and sausage shop. Like its flagship location, the stand serves chef Jeremy Nolen's regionally inspired traditional and modern German food. Wursthaus Schmitz features the best of Germany's imports, including mustards, vinegars, chocolates, rye bread and sauces, as well as a full line of hot sausage and schnitzel sandwiches, along with platters, cold sandwiches and freshly cut french fries. In addition to its hot offerings, Wursthaus sells house-made bratwurst, bauernwurst, Hungarian sausage and traditional German side dishes such as warm potato salad, sauerkraut, cucumber salad and red cabbage.

New to the Market is Hunger Burger, another venture by George Mickel.

Past Merchants of the Market

The Beer Garden, the Market's only watering hole for 25 years, served its last brew in 2011. Many customers and longtime merchants would meet there, bring their lunch and enjoy a glass or two.

Delilah's at the Terminal, owned by the vivacious Delilah Winder, was the Market's soul food center, serving up Southern-style favorites until its closing in 2012.

Many Market patrons remember Jill Horn, owner of Jill's Vorspeise, best known for her vegetarian specialties and incredible zucchini bread. Vorspeise was a part of the Market family for many years until its closing in 2002.

Tokyo Sushi closed its doors in 2014. David Dinh, who had been in the business for 32 years, will be missed by the many customers who enjoyed watching him expertly prepare sushi and sashimi.

Recipes that appeared in the first *Reading Terminal Market Cookbook* from Delilah's at the Terminal, Jill's Vorspeise and Tokyo Sushi remain in this new edition.

Avgolemono Soup with Chicken

Avgolemono is a Greek soup made with an egg-lemon mixture. It adds a distinctive flavor and also acts as a thickener. This version comes from Olympia Gyro.

1 small Spanish onion, finely chopped
2 carrots, finely chopped
2 celery stalks, finely chopped
2 to 3 tablespoons olive oil
1½ quarts chicken broth (canned or homemade)
2 cups water

1½ pounds boneless, skinless chicken breast
½ cup long-grain rice or orzo
3 eggs
3 tablespoons lemon juice
1½ teaspoons salt
2 tablespoons finely chopped flat-leaf parsley
1 teaspoon lemon zest

In a large stock pot, cook onions, carrots and celery in olive oil until tender. Add chicken broth and water and bring to a simmer. Add chicken breasts and simmer for 15 to 20 minutes, or until cooked through. Skim off the foam while cooking. Remove chicken and cut into bite-sized pieces. Set aside.

Add rice or orzo to the broth and boil gently for 10 to 15 minutes, or until done; then reduce heat to low and add reserved chicken to pot.

In a small bowl, beat eggs, lemon juice and salt. Add a cup of the hot broth to the egg mixture very slowly, whisking constantly. (This will temper the egg mixture to warm through before adding it back to the pot and will prevent curdling of the egg.) Over low heat, pour the egg-broth mixture back into the pot and stir until the soup is slightly thickened. Add parsley and lemon zest. Serve.

Makes four servings

Beck's Bread Pudding

According to Bill Beck, owner of Beck's Cajun Café, this bread pudding is their most popular and talked-about dish at the Reading Terminal Market. As one customer commented, it's "slap you mama good." To which Bill added, "I could not agree more." Serve with ice cream, macerated fruit or, as they do at Beck's, with a whiskey sauce.

CUSTARD

12 eggs

2¾ cups light brown sugar

1 teaspoon cinnamon

Pinch of nutmeg

¾ teaspoon pure bourbon vanilla extract

8 cups heavy cream

2 cups whole milk

FAUX CARAMEL

2 tablespoons water

½ cup light brown sugar

3 tablespoons butter (reserve 1 tablespoon to grease bottom of baking pan)

1 pear (leave skin on)

8 cups ¾-inch cubed French bread with crust removed

¼ cup raisins or minced dried fruit

For custard, in a bowl, beat eggs to combine. Add remaining custard ingredients, mix well. Set aside.

To make faux caramel, in a saucepan, add water and brown sugar, and cook over medium heat until mixture starts to simmer. Stir continuously for one minute. Turn off heat, remove pan from stove and gently stir in 2 tablespoons of the butter. Set aside.

Grease a 12 × 9 × 1½-inch baking pan with the reserved tablespoon of butter.

Lay the pear down on a cutting board with the fat end toward you. Take a knife and slice slightly to the right of the center and to the right of the stem. (The goal here is to just miss the core so that you get all the useable flesh). After cutting you will have one flat side piece of pear. Repeat same cutting action three more times around core of pear. Slice the four pieces of pear into ⅛-inch-thick slices and place on bottom of greased baking pan.

Pour the faux caramel, while hot or at least warm, over the pears. If sauce has cooled too much and is not pliable, reheat gently. Place bread cubes evenly over the pear mixture, add custard and sprinkle with raisins. Push bread into the custard to moisten; repeat this three times over the next 20 minutes so the bread can absorb the custard mixture.

Preheat oven to 275 degrees.

Cook bread pudding for 2 hours, or until top is light brown and crispy. Serve warm.

Makes 12 servings

Beck's Cajun Café, offering New Orleans-style cuisine.

Beck's Train Wreck

Owner-chef Bill Beck opened Beck's Cajun Café at the Reading Terminal Market, which once housed the Philadelphia terminal of the Reading Railroad line. Beck couldn't resist giving a nod to his surroundings with the Train Wreck sandwich. Lovingly referred to as "what a cheesesteak wants to be when it grows up," it's a bold blend of meats, cheese, onions and Beck's own Creole mayonnaise on French bread. Since winning the Best of Philly award in 2011, it has continued to be one of Beck's most popular items. The Creole mayonnaise is an essential ingredient and is available at Beck's.

¾ tablespoon vegetable oil
½ cup medium diced Spanish onion
3 ounces andouille sausage, diced
3 ounces salami, julienned
6 ounces chipped steak

½ teaspoon Beck's Devil Dust (see Note below)
6 slices American cheese
2 8-inch French baguettes
3 tablespoons Beck's Creole Mayonnaise

Heat a large, nonstick sauté pan until hot. Add oil and onions. Sauté, making sure to stir often, for 5 to 10 minutes, or until onions are caramelized. Add andouille sausage, salami and chipped steak (pull steak apart as it is cooked). Stir mixture to blend together and continue to cook about 3 to 4 minutes. Mix in Beck's Devil Dust to season.

Spread meat mixture evenly in pan and top with cheese slices, turn off heat and cover with a lid for 30 seconds, or until cheese is melted.

Split baguettes and spread the inside with Beck's Creole Mayonnaise. Use a spatula or spoon to flip the mixture into the bread so that the cheese lies directly on the bread. Indulge!

Makes two sandwiches

Note: Beck's Devil Dust is a blend of paprika, white and black pepper, cayenne pepper, celery seed, garlic powder, onion powder, oregano, sweet basil, thyme and sea salt.

Buttermilk Pancakes with Raspberry Sauce

When Spataro's opened in 1947, buttermilk was the sought-after drink. The sign from their store, "Drink Buttermilk, Live Forever," remains in the Market to this day. Spataro's is now Spataro's Cheesesteaks. This recipe is from Alex Spataro, son of the current owner and grandson of the original owner. They still cook using a lot of buttermilk. For this recipe, Alex says to feel free to substitute blackberries or other seasonal fruit in the sauce.

RASPBERRY SAUCE
½ cup sugar
Juice of 1 lemon
½ cup water
4 cups raspberries
¼ cup 100% light amber maple
    syrup (more if needed)
½ cup Chambord liqueur

BUTTERMILK PANCAKES
1¼ cups all-purpose flour
2 tablespoons granulated sugar
1 teaspoon baking powder

1 teaspoon baking soda
Pinch of salt
1 egg
1½ cups buttermilk
¼ cup canola oil
Chocolate chips, optional
Blueberries or other sliced fruit,
    optional

Butter for cooking pancakes,
    additional for serving
Maple syrup

To make raspberry sauce, in a medium saucepan over medium heat, whisk together sugar, lemon juice and water until combined. Reduce heat to medium-low. Add raspberries, maple syrup and Chambord, and stir occasionally using a wooden spoon. For a thinner, more "boozy" sauce, simmer for 10 minutes, stirring frequently. For a thicker, sweeter sauce, simmer for 15 minutes, stirring frequently until most of the berries have broken down. Add additional maple syrup as desired to sweeten sauce to taste.

Remove saucepan from heat and, using a fine mesh strainer placed over a bowl, strain seeds and remaining pulp from berries. Discard seeds and pulp. Let sauce cool about 10 minutes; it will thicken up a bit. Set aside. Any leftover sauce can be refrigerated for up to a week. Raspberry sauce is also great as a topping for ice cream.

To make pancakes, in a medium-sized bowl, whisk together all ingredients, adding chocolate chips and fruit, if desired. The consistency of the batter will be slightly thin.

Heat a skillet over medium heat. Coat bottom of skillet with butter (butter should be hot but not browned). Ladle batter into pan, forming circles about 6 inches wide. Cook until bubbles form and edges of pancakes are slightly firm. Flip with a spatula and cook other side. Pancakes should be lightly golden on both sides. Keep them warm if cooking in batches.

Serve with butter, maple syrup and reserved raspberry sauce.

Makes eight six-inch pancakes

Domenic Spataro, owner of Spataro's, established in 1947,
now offers hoagies, cheesesteaks and sandwiches.

Buttermilk Wheat Bread

This recipe is from Domenic C. Spataro, the original owner of Spataro's in the Market. When he first opened his stand, he sold a lot of buttermilk. People would ask for a glass along with their sandwich. Buttermilk was originally made from the residue left over from butter-making, with butter granules added. Today, buttermilk is produced from pasteurized skim milk and a culture is added to develop flavor and consistency. Buttermilk is lower in fat and more easily digested than whole milk. This buttermilk wheat bread is simply delicious.

Butter or vegetable oil for greasing
    pan
2½ cups buttermilk
2½ teaspoons baking soda
4 tablespoons (½ stick) butter,
    softened

½ cup sugar
1 extra-large egg
1½ cups all-purpose flour
2¼ cups whole wheat flour

Preheat oven to 350 degrees.

Use the butter or oil to grease two standard 8-inch loaf pans.

In a bowl, mix buttermilk and baking soda until soda has dissolved. Set aside.

In another bowl, cream together butter and sugar. Stir in egg and mix well. Add the buttermilk mixture to the creamed butter. Gradually stir both flours into the batter and mix until ingredients are just blended. Do not overmix.

Divide between the prepared pans and bake for approximately 1 hour. The bread is done when a toothpick inserted in center comes out dry. Remove bread from oven and cool for 5 to 10 minutes. Turn loaves out of pan onto a rack and cool completely.

Makes two loaves

Carmen's "The Classic" Cheesesteak

Of the numerous cheesesteaks and toppings available at Carmen's Famous Hoagies and Cheesesteaks, "The Classic" is their top seller. "Only the best-quality rib eye is used," says Carmen DiGuglielmo, the owner. "Our meat comes from a company in Kansas, and is specially cut to meet our specifications." Great ingredients are the key to this classic sandwich.

8 ounces thinly shaved rib eye
¼ cup sliced onion
¼ cup sliced fresh white button
  mushrooms

Roasted peppers (hot, sweet or a
  combination of both), as desired
1 10-inch hoagie roll
¼ cup Cheez Whiz

In a skillet over medium heat, add onion, mushrooms and peppers. Sauté a few minutes, or until lightly browned. To same skillet, add rib eye and continue sautéing until meat is no longer pink.

Slice open roll and spread with Cheez Whiz. (If you prefer more cheese flavor, add Cheez Whiz to meat mixture in skillet.)

Fill roll with steak mixture and let sit a minute, so Cheez Whiz can blend with other ingredients.

Makes one cheesesteak

Chicken Korma

Nanee's Kitchen, started by Tayyaba Khanum and her sister Khalida, is a family business now managed by their nephew Da'nish and his wife Sabina. In their new expanded location, Nanee's Kitchen specializes in gluten-free, vegan and vegetarian dishes, although meat and fish dishes are offered as well. Traditional grocery items are available, along with Nanee's special spice mix. Here is a popular recipe that both children and adults will enjoy.

¼ cup vegetable oil

1 large onion, chopped

1 pound boneless chicken breasts, cubed

½ teaspoon fresh ginger, finely chopped

1 teaspoon garlic, finely chopped

1 teaspoon garam masala

½ teaspoon red chili powder

¼ teaspoon turmeric powder

1 tablespoon ground almonds

1 tablespoon ground cashews

1 tablespoon tomato paste

½ cup plain yogurt

Salt to taste

In a sauté pan over low heat, add oil and lightly brown onions for about 5 minutes.

Raise heat to medium and add cubed chicken, ginger, garlic, garam masala, red chili powder, ground turmeric, almonds and cashews. Stir to mix thoroughly. Add the tomato paste, stir, lower heat and cook for 15 to 20 minutes, or until chicken is cooked through. Do not overcook.

Add yogurt and salt to taste. Mix well and serve.

Makes four servings

Chili Dogs

According to Russell Black, owner of Franks A-Lot, using top-quality hot dogs and unusual toppings makes the difference. Franks A-Lot also serves barbecued chicken, homemade hamburgers, kielbasa sausages and incredible cheese cornbread. The addition of beer and coffee in this dish gives it a boost. The chili can also be served in bowls. (The recipe makes about four bowl-size servings.)

1 tablespoon vegetable oil
1 large onion, sliced
1 green pepper, sliced
2 garlic cloves, minced
1 pound ground beef
Salt and freshly ground pepper to
   taste

¾ cup draft beer
1 cup tomato sauce
1 to 2 tablespoons freshly brewed
   coffee
1 tablespoon chili powder
12 hot dogs, boiled or grilled
12 hot dog rolls

Place the oil in a medium skillet and cook the onion, pepper and garlic over low heat until softened, about 10 minutes. Add ground beef and cook until well browned. Season with salt and pepper. Add beer, tomato sauce, coffee and chili powder, then cook about 20 to 30 minutes, stirring often, until thickened.

Place hot dogs in rolls, top with chili, and serve.

Makes enough chili to top 12 hot dogs

Crêpes

Crêpes can be made in minutes and make an impressive presentation. They are versatile and can be served for almost any meal, including dessert. When making crêpes, it's well worth doubling the quantity, as they freeze beautifully. Lunch and dinner crêpes are often filled with cooked chicken, vegetables and cheese. Dessert crêpes can be filled with various fruits and topped with your favorite dessert sauce. This recipe is from Blerim, manager of Profi's Crêperie. He suggests getting creative with your own fillings. At Profi's Crêperie, a popular one is Nutella, banana and strawberries.

2 eggs
2 teaspoon sugar
1 teaspoon salt

1¼ tablespoon butter, softened
½ cup reduced fat milk
About 1 cup flour

In a bowl or blender, combine the eggs, sugar, salt, butter and milk, then blend until smooth. Add in the flour until the mixture resembles a thickened batter.

Lightly butter a small skillet or crêpe maker over medium heat. Pour about ¼ cup of batter into skillet, then tilt it in a circular motion so that the batter coats the surface evenly. Cook crêpe for about 1½ minutes until the bottom is lightly golden. Loosen with a spatula, flip over and cook the other side for about 1 minute. Continue with the remaining batter. Serve with your favorite filling.

Makes approximately eight crêpes

Delilah's Old-Fashioned Banana Pudding

Delilah's at the Terminal was a Reading Terminal Market restaurant for many moons. This recipe appeared in our first Market cookbook. Delilah Winder grew up eating her godmother's puddings. This banana pudding was a favorite at Delilah's.

2 tablespoons butter	2 teaspoons vanilla extract
¾ cup sugar	Zest from ½ lemon
3 eggs, lightly beaten	1 12-ounce box vanilla wafers
1 cup milk	6 ripe bananas, sliced
1½ teaspoons all-purpose flour	6 egg whites

Preheat oven to 350 degrees.

Make a sauce by placing the butter, ½ cup of the sugar, the eggs, milk, flour, vanilla and lemon zest in a medium saucepan over low heat. Cook until thickened.

In a 13 × 9 × 2-inch baking pan, place a layer of wafers, cover with sliced bananas and pour the sauce over mixture.

In a bowl, beat egg whites until stiff, gradually add the remaining ¼ cup sugar, and beat until a smooth meringue forms. Pour the meringue evenly over the banana mixture and bake for 20 to 25 minutes, or until meringue is lightly browned. Serve hot or at room temperature.

Makes four to six servings

Delilah's Southern Fried Chicken

This recipe appears to use a lot of hot pepper sauce, but the heat mellows considerably during the marinating process. The result adds just enough pep to this traditional Southern fried chicken. Delilah Winder, once the owner of Delilah's at the Terminal, served outstanding fried chicken and cornbread. We include her recipe, which appeared in the first edition of *The Reading Terminal Market Cookbook,* even though Delilah's is no longer in the Market. Delilah is partial to Crystal hot sauce from Louisiana, and she recommends using canola oil for frying.

1 6-ounce bottle Crystal brand hot sauce

1 frying chicken, cut into parts

Flour for dredging

½ teaspoon salt

Canola oil for frying

Place hot sauce in a large bowl, and marinate chicken pieces for several hours.

Combine flour and salt in a plastic bag. Place chicken parts in bag and shake well to coat with mixture.

In a deep skillet, add enough oil to come three-quarters of the way up the sides. Fry the chicken, covered, for about 15 minutes, then uncover and continue frying for another 5 to 10 minutes, or until chicken is cooked through and nicely browned.

Makes four servings

Down Home Diner's Cheese Grits

Grits are a favorite Southern food, and popular at the Market's Down Home Diner. Hominy grits are ground, hulled corn, white in color and mild in flavor. Grits are usually served with eggs, but can be used with casseroles.

1 cup quick grits
2½ cups shredded cheddar cheese
¼ pound (1 stick) butter, softened
½ cup milk

Generous dash of hot pepper sauce
Pinch of garlic salt
2 eggs, beaten

Preheat oven to 350 degrees.

Grease a 2-quart casserole.

Cook grits according to package directions. Place the grits in a large saucepan and add 1½ cups of the cheese, butter, milk, hot pepper sauce and garlic salt. Cook over low heat until cheese has melted. Remove from heat and stir in the beaten eggs.

Pour mixture into the prepared pan, sprinkle with the remaining cheese and bake for 45 minutes to 1 hour, or until set.

Makes six servings

The neon sign at the Down Home Diner.

Fillet of Beef Yucatan

The tortillas sold at the 12th Street Cantina are made with stone-ground white corn, not from a mix. The consistency of their tortillas is more traditional, a little thicker and tastier than the commercial ones.

1 garlic bulb
4 cloves
1 teaspoon dried thyme
3 allspice berries
½ teaspoon black peppercorns
½ teaspoon cumin seeds
1 tablespoon cider vinegar

1 teaspoon honey
½ teaspoon salt
4 5-ounce steak fillets
2 tablespoons corn oil
12 (1 package) 6-inch corn tortillas, warmed

Preheat oven to 325 degrees.

Place the garlic bulb in a small baking pan and roast until softened, about 30 to 40 minutes. Squeeze the garlic out of the skins and reserve.

Meanwhile, in a dry skillet over medium heat, lightly toast the cloves, thyme, all-spice berries, black peppercorns and cumin seeds. Toss the spices a few times to brown them evenly. Reduce heat if needed. Be careful not to burn.

Finely grind the spices and place them in a small bowl. Add the reserved garlic to the spices and, with a fork, mash into a paste. Add vinegar, honey and salt. Marinate steaks in this paste for 3 to 6 hours. Brush steaks with corn oil and grill to desired doneness. Slice and wrap in warm tortillas.

Makes four servings

Fire-Roasted Chicken with Feta and Greek Olives

Mezze restaurant has been at the Reading Terminal Market for more than 10 years. Its owners, George and Kim Mickel, also own By George Pasta, Pizza and Cheesesteak, which is in its second decade of operation. This flavorful chicken recipe came from Mezze Mediterranean Foods.

MARINADE
2 tablespoons olive oil
1 teaspoon lemon juice
½ teaspoon garlic
¼ teaspoon paprika
⅛ teaspoon salt
¼ teaspoon pepper

2 boneless, skinless chicken breasts
3 plum tomatoes, seeded and
 chopped
3 tablespoons feta cheese, crumbled
3 tablespoons sliced Kalamata olives
1 tablespoon minced parsley for
 garnish

To make marinade, in a nonreactive bowl, combine olive oil, lemon juice, garlic, paprika, salt and pepper. Place chicken breasts in marinade. Refrigerate overnight.

Prepare grill and preheat oven to 350 degrees.

Remove chicken from marinade, and reserve the marinade. Grill chicken breasts for 8 to 10 minutes, or until just done. Slice chicken and place in a shallow, oven-proof baking pan. Heat reserved marinade, then pour over chicken. Top with tomatoes, feta cheese and olives.

Place in oven for about 3 to 4 minutes to soften feta. Sprinkle with parsley and serve.

Makes two servings

Guacamole

No party is complete without a bowl of guacamole and tortilla chips. This version comes from Michelle Leff of 12th Street Cantina. If you prefer a creamier version, prepare it in a food processor or blender by processing all ingredients together until smooth. Guacamole is best prepared shortly before serving to prevent the avocado from discoloring. To help ripen avocados, place them in a brown paper bag and let them sit at room temperature for a few days.

4 medium-sized ripe avocados,
    peeled and sliced
1 tomato, diced
¼ cup finely chopped onion
1 garlic clove, minced
½ teaspoon paprika

Juice of 1 lime
1 to 2 jalapeño peppers, seeded and
    chopped
Salt and freshly ground black
    pepper to taste

In a large bowl, mash the avocados with a fork. Add remaining ingredients and combine thoroughly. This method produces a slightly chunky version.

Makes about two cups

Hershel's East Side Deli Cabbage Borsht

This recipe, provided by Steven Safern, owner of Hershel's East Side Deli, is a great, hearty dish for large family gatherings. Steven remembers his mother, who was born in Czechoslovakia, making what she called "peasant soup" to feed the entire family. If serving a smaller group, freeze the remaining unused soup. Steven says that leftover brisket from another meal can be used and will do just fine. To make a vegetarian version, eliminate the brisket and substitute vegetable stock.

6 tablespoons vegetable oil
2 large onions, thinly sliced
1 cup apple cider vinegar
1 cup brown sugar
1 teaspoon crushed red pepper
10 cups chicken stock

2 cups crushed tomatoes
3 pounds brisket, chopped
1 large head of cabbage, coarsely
  chopped
10 medium red bliss potatoes,
  medium diced

In a large stock pot, add oil and heat over medium heat. Add onion and cook, stirring occasionally, until onion is soft, about 10 minutes. Add vinegar, brown sugar and crushed red pepper, then stir. Add chicken stock and crushed tomatoes, brisket and cabbage, and bring to a boil. Turn down heat and simmer for 45 minutes. Add potatoes and continue to cook for an additional 45 minutes. Cool soup and skim off fat. Reheat to serve.

Makes 10 to 12 servings

Hummus

Tahini, a paste made from sesame seeds, has a strong, nutty flavor. Lemon salt, another ingredient used in the recipe, can be purchased from Kamal's Middle Eastern Specialties and is used in many dishes from the Arab world. You can make your own by combining one tablespoon of sea salt with the finely minced zest of one lemon.

2 cups canned chickpeas, drained
    and rinsed
3 garlic cloves, smashed
½ cup tahini

1 teaspoon lemon salt, or to taste
½ to 1 cup water
Pita bread, cut into wedges

Place the chickpeas and garlic in the bowl of a food processor fitted with a steel blade and blend. Add the tahini and lemon salt, and process until just blended. With the machine running, gradually add water until mixture is smooth and creamy. Chill for several hours, bring to room temperature, and serve with pita wedges.

Makes about two cups

Moroccan chicken from Kamal's Middle Eastern Specialties *(see page 166)*.

LEFT: Pad Thai goong sod from Little Thai Market (see pages 167–168).

RIGHT: Oyster stew from Pearl's Oyster Bar (see page 171).

ABOVE: Pepperoni stromboli from By George Pizza, Pasta and Cheese-steaks *(see page 172).*

LEFT: Honey and spiced pears from Iovine Brothers Produce *(see page 116).*

ABOVE: DiNic's pulled pork sandwich *(see pages 181–182)*.

LEFT: Vegetable lasagna with tomato cream sauce from By George Pizza, Pasta and Cheesesteaks *(see pages 185–186)*.

Meat Loaf

This recipe is from Tootsie's Salad Express. Tootsie's chef, Betty Thompson, likes to use dark soy sauce because of its rich and robust flavor. She says it is a good ingredient to have in home cupboards. Betty uses it when she makes meat loaf as well as when she prepares gravy for some of her other dishes.

2 pounds ground beef	**GRAVY**
1 green pepper, grated	4 cups water
2 cloves garlic, minced	2 beef bouillon cubes
1 medium onion, finely chopped	¼ teaspoon freshly grated black
2 tablespoons steak sauce	pepper
1 tablespoon chopped parsley	1 tablespoon cornstarch
¼ cup bread crumbs	1 tablespoon dark soy sauce
1 large egg, beaten	

Preheat oven to 350 degrees.

Grease a standard loaf pan.

In a large bowl, thoroughly mix the beef, green pepper, garlic, onion, steak sauce, parsley, bread crumbs, and beaten egg. Place in the prepared loaf pan, and bake for 1 hour.

To make the gravy, place the water, bouillon cubes and pepper into a saucepan, bring to a boil, reduce heat and cook until the cubes have dissolved. Sift in the cornstarch and cook until thickened, about 3 to 4 minutes. Add the soy sauce and stir well. Serve meat loaf with gravy.

Makes six to eight servings

Mediterranean Tortellini Salad

This simply prepared pasta salad came from Mezze Mediterranean Foods. A no-mayonnaise salad, it is excellent for outdoor picnics. It also makes a colorful addition to any dinner or buffet. The roasted pepper pesto and cherry-size mozzarella are available at By George Pasta, Pizza and Cheesesteak.

1 pound tortellini pasta
1 cup broccoli rabe
1 cup cherry-size fresh mozzarella, cut in half
1 tablespoon chopped fresh basil
½ pint cherry tomatoes, cut in half
¼ cup Italian salad dressing
½ cup roasted pepper pesto

1 tablespoon lemon juice
Salt and pepper to taste
1 tablespoon chopped parsley
1 tablespoon chopped garlic
¼ cup olive oil
¼ cup freshly grated Parmesan cheese

Cook pasta according to package directions.

In a saucepan, bring water to a boil and cook broccoli rabe about 4 minutes. Plunge into an ice-water bath, drain and chop.

In a large bowl, combine pasta, broccoli rabe and remaining ingredients. Toss and serve.

Makes four to six servings

Michelle's Shrimp Enchiladas

Michelle Leff, owner of the 12th Street Cantina, offers a primer on ingredients frequently found in Mexican dishes. Poblano chilies are dark green and about five inches long, tapering to a point. They are medium hot and have a wonderful, smoky flavor when roasted. Serrano chilies are bright green or red; about two inches long, and are hot but not bitter—great for making salsas. Tomatillos are yellowish-green with papery husks that should be removed before using the fruit. When raw, they are quite tart, but they have a milder, lemony flavor when cooked. And here's a tip for taking some of the heat out of chilies: Slice them lengthwise, then remove the rib and seeds.

12 poblano chilies
3 tablespoons olive oil
5 garlic cloves, minced
1 small onion, diced
2 pounds medium shrimp, shelled and deveined
6 ears corn, removed from the cob, or 5 cups canned corn
½ teaspoon Mexican oregano
5 sprigs fresh cilantro, chopped
2 fresh serrano chilies
Salt and freshly ground pepper to taste

GREEN ENCHILADA SAUCE
10 tomatillos, husks removed
4 garlic cloves, minced
2 serrano chilies
1 medium onion, chopped
Salt and black pepper to taste
2 teaspoons Mexican oregano
2 tablespoons vegetable oil, plus more for dipping tortillas
10 sprigs fresh cilantro, chopped
Pinch of sugar

12 fresh corn tortillas
2 cups sour cream or crème fraiche

Cook poblano chilies over an open flame, or broil them until charred. Place in a paper bag for about 10 minutes. Remove from bag, peel skin from each chili, and cut into strips. Reserve half of chilies for green enchilada sauce. Set aside.

In a skillet, heat oil. Add garlic and onion, and sauté 1 to 2 minutes. Add shrimp, corn and half of the poblano chilies, then cook another 2 to 3 minutes. Add oregano and cilantro, remove from heat, add serrano chilies and season with salt and pepper. Set aside.

To make green enchilada sauce, in a large saucepan, bring water to a boil, blanch tomatillos for about 15 minutes, and drain. In a blender or food processor fitted with a steel blade, place the tomatillos, garlic, remaining poblano chilies, serrano chilies, onion, salt, pepper and Mexican oregano. Blend until smooth. Set aside. In a small saucepan, heat 2 tablespoons vegetable oil, add the tomatillo mixture, reduce heat and simmer for about 20 minutes. Add cilantro and sugar. Remove from heat and reserve.

Preheat oven to 325 degrees.

Prepare enchiladas: Heat 1 inch of oil in a medium skillet. Hold the fresh tortillas with tongs and dip quickly into the hot oil for 5 to 10 seconds. Drain on paper towels.

Dip each tortilla into the reserved enchilada sauce and place a portion of the shrimp mixture on one side of each tortilla. Fold each tortilla in half and place them on two baking sheets. Cover the sheets with foil, place in oven, and heat through for approximately 10 minutes.

Remove and serve topped with sour cream or crème fraiche.

Makes 12 servings

The 12th Street Cantina.

Miso Bean Soup with Tofu and Seaweed

Miso is an inspired Japanese culinary favorite made by boiling soybeans, mashing them and adding rice, wheat or barley in different proportions and then fermenting. Store unused tofu in the refrigerator in plenty of cold water (change the water daily). The tofu and the fermented flavors are the basis for this classic soup, which used to be served at Tokyo Sushi.

6 cups water
1 sheet kamu seaweed, cut into strips

3 tablespoons white miso
½ pound soft tofu, diced
2 scallions, chopped for garnish

In a large saucepan, bring water to a boil. Remove from heat, add the seaweed and soak until softened. Remove seaweed, reserving broth and seaweed.

In a small bowl, make a paste by mixing the miso with 2 tablespoons of the reserved broth. Bring the reserved broth to a simmer and gradually stir in miso paste until dissolved. Add tofu and simmer gently for a few minutes. Do not bring to a boil.

Ladle into hot soup bowls and garnish with chopped scallions and reserved seaweed, which has a slightly salty, fishy flavor.

Makes four servings

Moroccan Chicken

The spice mixture in this recipe from Kamal's Middle Eastern Specialties is made in a quantity far larger than what you'll need. The unused portion freezes well and can be used in other recipes. A lot of liquid will remain after roasting. Reserve that liquid and use it as a base for soups or for cooking rice.

2 bunches flat-leaf parsley
1 medium onion, quartered
¼ cup garlic powder
2 tablespoons ground coriander
2 tablespoons ground ginger

1 tablespoon black pepper
Salt to taste
2 chickens, 3 to 3½ pounds each
Fresh coriander for garnish

In a food processor or blender, process the parsley and onion. Add garlic powder, ground coriander, ground ginger, black pepper and salt, and blend to a smooth paste.

Preheat oven to 350 degrees.

Spread ½ cup of the spice mixture on the bottom of a large baking pan. (Reserve remaining mixture for another recipe.) Place chicken on top and add enough water to come up sides of chicken. Bake uncovered for approximately 1½ hours, or until chicken is very tender. Cut chicken into serving pieces and place on a platter with some of the pan juices. Garnish with fresh coriander.

Makes eight servings

Pad Thai Goong Sod
(Fried Rice Sticks with Shrimp)

Pad Thai is one of Thailand's popular national dishes and is served at Little Thai Market, owned by Tak and Kaysone Lam. Most of the ingredients used in this recipe are available from their stand. Tamarind plays an important part in Asian, Mexican and Indian cookery, and it is used in a great many chutneys, curries and sauces. It is a sticky, sour-tasting fruit that grows in large brown pods on the tamarind tree. Palm sugar, another important ingredient in this dish, is a natural and unrefined sugar that resembles brown sugar but has more of a caramel and butterscotch flavor. Palm sugar comes in the form of a paste and is sold in jars.

SAUCE
3 tablespoons palm sugar
3 tablespoons fish sauce
3 tablespoons tamarind pulp, soaked in warm water to soften, then strained to remove seeds and fiber

6 medium shrimp, shelled and deveined
5 tablespoons vegetable oil
1 cake pressed bean curd, diced
5 garlic cloves, minced
5 shallots, minced

1 tablespoon dried shrimp or prawns, soaked in warm water for 5 minutes, then drained
1 tablespoon pickled radish
10 ounces dried rice-stick noodles, soaked in ½ cup warm water for about 5 minutes
Dried red pepper flakes to taste
3 eggs, lightly beaten
2 cups bean sprouts, rinsed
¼ cup garlic chives or spring onions, sliced in 1-inch lengths
2 tablespoons crushed peanuts
Sprig of cilantro

To make the sauce, place in a small saucepan palm sugar, fish sauce, and 3 tablespoons of the juice from the tamarind pulp and bring to a boil. Reduce heat and simmer for 3 to 5 minutes. Remove from heat and set aside.

Grill or broil shrimp and set aside.

Heat 3 tablespoons of the oil in a large saucepan. Add bean curd and stir-fry until lightly brown, about 5 minutes. Drain and set aside.

In the same pan, stir-fry garlic and shallots over high heat for 2 minutes. Add hydrated shrimp and pickled radish, and fry for another 3 minutes. Add noodles and bean curd, then stir-fry to mix. Add the sauce mixture and red pepper flakes. Continue to stir-fry over medium heat for another 1 to 2 minutes.

Push noodle mixture to one side. Add the remaining 2 tablespoons of oil to the pan, then add the eggs and scramble until lightly cooked. Mix the eggs and noodles together. Toss in half the bean sprouts and the garlic chives or spring onions. Mix together thoroughly and remove from heat.

Serve garnished with the remaining bean sprouts, crushed peanuts and grilled shrimp. Place a sprig of cilantro on top.

Makes four servings

The sign above the Little Thai Market.

Peach-Glazed Ham Chops with Summer Green Bean Salad

This recipe from Molly Malloy's is a reflection of the restaurant's innovative dishes using the freshest produce available. They recommend using "summer" peaches. Of course, the produce is provided by Iovine Brothers Produce, owned by Jimmy and Vinnie Iovine, who also own Molly Malloy's. It is named in honor of their mother.

GREEN BEAN SALAD

1 pound fresh green beans, stems removed
1 pint grape tomatoes
¼ Bermuda onion, thinly sliced
1 bunch mint, julienned
1 lemon, zest and juiced
2 tablespoons olive oil
Salt and pepper to taste

HAM CHOPS WITH PEACHES

1 teaspoon canola oil
4 6-ounce ham chops
½ cup thinly sliced Bermuda onion
1 garlic clove, minced
2 ripe peaches, peeled, pitted and sliced
¼ teaspoon red chili flakes
⅛ teaspoon cracked black pepper
1 teaspoon brown sugar
2 tablespoons white balsamic vinegar
Salt to taste

To make green bean salad, bring a pot of water to a boil. Add green beans and cook for about 1 minute (they will still be crisp). Drain green beans and place into an ice bath (cold water with a couple cubes of ice). Drain beans again, place in a bowl and mix with remaining ingredients. Refrigerate until ready to serve.

To make ham chops with peaches, heat a 12-inch skillet until hot. Add canola oil and ham chops. Cook about 1 minute and flip chops over. Add onions, garlic and peaches, and sauté for another minute. Add remaining ingredients and cook 2 to 4 minutes longer, or until chops are glazed. Sprinkle with salt.

To serve, place desired amount of green bean salad on a plate, top with ham chop and, as Molly Malloy's puts it, spread the love with the peach and onion mixture.

Makes four servings

Pearl's Fried Oysters

Pearl's Oyster Bar has been serving fried oysters for over 60 years. Their counter is filled with customers who are always in the mood for a great, crispy platter of oysters or fish. For this recipe, Pearl's chef Rob Swinton prefers using bread crumbs to coat the oysters. He says that they give a lighter coating than cracker crumbs.

Oil for frying
Flour for dredging
2 eggs
⅓ cup milk

Salt and freshly ground pepper to
    taste
2 cups bread crumbs
25 large oysters
Lemon wedges for garnish

In a deep skillet or fryer, pour in enough oil to come halfway up the sides of the skillet. Heat oil until hot. (The oil is at the proper temperature when a piece of bread sizzles on contact and browns in a few seconds.)

Meanwhile, place flour on a shallow plate. In a bowl, whisk together the eggs, milk, salt and pepper. Place bread crumbs on another shallow plate. Lightly flour the oysters, dip them into the egg mixture, then drain off excess batter and coat with bread crumbs.

Fry the oysters until browned, turning them over once or twice during cooking. Drain on paper towels. Garnish with lemon wedges and serve.

Makes four servings

Pearl's Oyster Stew

Rob Swinton of Pearl's Oyster Bar shares his tip for making a good oyster stew, one of winter's pleasures. He suggests cooking the oysters and milk separately, then combining. Oyster stew is traditionally served with oyster crackers.

2 to 3 pints medium shucked
   oysters
6 cups whole milk

1 tablespoon butter
Paprika for garnish

In a saucepan, gently cook the oysters in their juices until the edges are slightly curled, about 2 to 3 minutes. In another saucepan, heat milk just to a boil and gradually pour it over the oysters. Add butter and stir. Ladle into soup bowls and sprinkle paprika on top of each serving.

Makes four servings

*Pearl's Oyster Bar, well-known for oyster stew
and fresh seafood platters.*

Pepperoni Stromboli

Using already prepared bread dough that is available from By George Pizza, Pasta & Cheesesteaks makes this recipe quick and easy, and it can be assembled in no time at all. George Mickel, the owner of By George, suggests varying the filling according to taste and preference.

1½ pounds bread dough	Oil for greasing baking sheet
8 ounces shredded mozzarella cheese	Oil for brushing
¼ pound pepperoni, thinly sliced	1 tablespoon sesame seeds

Preheat oven to 450 degrees.

Cut dough in half and stretch one piece into a round that is 9 inches in diameter. Place half the shredded mozzarella down the center of the dough and top with half the pepperoni slices. Fold one side over the filling, overlap with the other side, tuck in the end and, using your fingers, pinch all the seams securely to seal. Repeat with the other piece of dough and the remaining mozzarella and pepperoni. Place seam side down on a greased baking sheet, brush with oil and sprinkle with sesame seeds.

Bake for 15 to 20 minutes, or until golden brown. Remove from oven, let cool for 5 minutes and cut into 1-inch-thick slices to serve.

Makes about 18 slices

Roula's Greek Salad Sandwich

Tzatziki makes a wonderfully refreshing spread for this sandwich based on the popular Greek salad. Roula Voulgaridis of Olympia Gyro created this special sandwich.

TZATZIKI
1 cup minced seedless cucumber
2 garlic cloves
1 tablespoon chopped fresh dill
½ cup plain Greek yogurt
¼ cup sour cream
Salt and pepper to taste

DRESSING
2 tablespoons red wine vinegar
3 to 4 tablespoons finely chopped
    flat-leaf parsley
½ teaspoon oregano

Salt and pepper to taste
¼ cup extra virgin olive oil

SALAD FILLING
1 cup thinly sliced baby spinach
1 cup sliced seedless cucumber
1¼ cups halved grape tomatoes
½ cup pitted and chopped Kalamata
    olives
½ cup thinly sliced radishes
1½ cups feta cheese, crumbled

6 whole wheat pita breads

To make tzatziki, place the minced cucumber in a kitchen towel and squeeze out as much liquid as possible. Set aside.

In a food processor, combine garlic, dill, yogurt and sour cream, then blend until smooth. Put mixture into a bowl and add reserved minced cucumber. Stir well. Add salt and pepper to taste. Set tzatziki aside.

To make dressing, combine vinegar, parsley, oregano, salt and pepper in a small bowl. Whisk in the olive oil. Set aside.

To make salad filling, in a bowl, combine spinach, cucumber, tomatoes, olives and radishes. Toss with the dressing, add feta at the end and toss once more.

To make sandwiches, spread tzatziki in each pita and fill with the dressed salad. Serve.

Makes six sandwiches

Roula's Revani

This recipe comes from Roula Voulgaridis of Olympia Gyro. It is a classic Greek dessert soaked in simple sugar syrup. The addition of shredded coconut gives it an interesting twist. Revani is a nice alternative to the more popular baklava.

6 large eggs
1½ cups sugar
1 cup canola oil
½ cup milk (whole or 2%)
½ teaspoon vanilla extract
2 cups all-purpose flour
4 teaspoons baking powder
1½ cups shredded coconut

Nonstick baking spray for greasing pan

SYRUP
2 cups sugar
2 cups water
½ whole lemon

Preheat oven to 350 degrees.

Grease a 13 × 9 × 1½-inch baking pan with nonstick spray. Set aside.

In a large bowl, beat eggs, sugar, oil, milk and vanilla until well combined.

In another bowl, sift flour and baking powder together.

Add the dry ingredients to the wet ingredients and beat until mixture is well combined. Add the coconut and stir.

Spread the batter evenly into prepared pan. Bake for 1 hour, or until a toothpick inserted in center comes out clean.

While cake is baking, make syrup. In a saucepan, combine sugar, water and lemon. Bring to a boil, reduce heat to low and cook for about 30 minutes, or until slightly thickened. Remove and discard lemon. Let syrup cool.

When cake is done, cut it while still hot into squares, then cut the squares diagonally to create triangular pieces.

Slowly add the syrup to the warm cake, using one ladle at a time. Let the cake cool so that all the syrup is absorbed.

Makes eight to 10 servings

Sesame Noodles

Noodles symbolize longevity in China, and come in various shapes and sizes, fresh or dry. American or Italian packaged noodles can be used as a substitute in this recipe. All Chinese noodle dishes begin with boiled noodles, which are rinsed in cold water to remove the starch and are drained well before final cooking. Sang Kee Peking Duck prepares several noodle dishes, and this is one of the best.

1 pound Chinese noodles, fresh or dried	Dash of chili oil
1 12-ounce jar sesame paste	Pinch of sugar
¼ cup sesame oil	1 cup shredded Chinese cabbage
¼ cup soy sauce	1 cup shredded carrots
¼ cup oyster sauce	1 red pepper, thinly sliced
¼ cup red wine vinegar	1 tablespoon rice wine vinegar

Bring a large pot of water to a boil and cook noodles. Drain and let cool.

In a bowl, combine sesame paste, sesame oil, soy sauce, oyster sauce, red wine vinegar, chili oil and sugar. Pour mixture over noodles and toss well. Place on a serving dish.

Combine cabbage, carrots and red pepper in a bowl. Mix in rice wine vinegar and toss well. Place vegetables over noodles and serve at room temperature.

Makes four servings

Spataro's Cream Cheese and Olive Sandwich

The "Old Style" cream cheese and olive sandwich first appeared on Spataro's menu when they opened in the 1940s. It remains on the menu of what is now Spataro's Cheesesteaks to this day. Owner Domenic Mark Spataro, son of the original owner, admits that the Philly cheesesteak is the most popular sandwich they serve, followed by their stacked corned beef special. The cream cheese and olive sandwich is still fun to make. It's moist and very tasty, and is enjoyed by grown-ups and children alike.

2 slices rye or whole-wheat bread
2 ounces cream cheese
2 tablespoons chopped green olives
    with pimentos

2 lettuce leaves
2 to 3 tomato slices

Spread both pieces of bread with cream cheese. Layer one side with olives, lettuce and tomato. Top with second slice of bread. Cut in half and enjoy.

Makes one sandwich

Stuffed Zucchini

The use of cinnamon, fresh mint and pine nuts is traditional in many Middle Eastern dishes. Kamal Albarouki of Kamal's Middle Eastern Specialties suggests using this stuffing for other vegetables, such as peppers or eggplants.

1 pound ground lamb or beef
2 tablespoons pine nuts, toasted
1 medium onion, finely chopped
½ teaspoon ground cinnamon
2 tablespoons olive oil
2½ pounds ripe tomatoes, chopped

2 garlic cloves, minced
2 tablespoons chopped fresh mint
Salt and freshly ground pepper to taste
6 small zucchini, halved lengthwise, flesh scooped out

Preheat oven to 350 degrees.

In a bowl, combine meat, pine nuts, onion and cinnamon. Heat the oil in a medium skillet over medium heat. Add the meat mixture and sauté for 10 minutes, or until meat is well browned and the onion has softened. With a spatula, break up meat in pan while sautéing.

In a large bowl, combine the chopped tomatoes with their juices, the garlic, mint, salt and pepper.

Place the zucchini halves side by side in a large baking pan and stuff each piece with a portion of the meat mixture. Press down gently to even the filling. Pour tomato mixture over and around the zucchini, then bake for 25 to 30 minutes, or until zucchini are tender.

Makes six servings

Sushi

Sushi-making is an art in Japan, requiring many years of apprenticeship before one is declared to have mastered it. Sushi means "vinegared rice," and depending on local products, each region has its own specialty. Of the many varieties of seaweed, nori is the most common and is available in dark-green sheets. Wasabi is a very hot paste, similar in taste to horseradish, made from the powdered root of the wasabi plant. You can buy it prepared, or you can mix a small amount of water with a little wasabi powder and stir until smooth. This recipe came from David Dinh, who once owned The Sushi Bar.

2¼ cups Japanese sushi rice, or
   short-grained white rice
2¼ cups water
¼ cup Japanese rice wine vinegar
6 sheets of nori

6 ounces smoked salmon or smoked
   bluefish, evenly sliced, about
   ⅛-inch thick
Pickled ginger, for garnish
Wasabi, for garnish

Rinse rice several times in plenty of cold water; drain and set aside in a bowl for about 30 minutes.

Place rice in a heavy saucepan or steamer and add 2¼ cups of water. Bring just to a simmer, cover with a tight-fitting lid and cook about 20 to 25 minutes. If you're using a steamer, follow the manufacturer's instructions. When the rice is done, remove it from the heat, place it in a bowl, cover with a cloth or paper towel and let it sit for 10 minutes.

Drizzle the rice wine vinegar over the rice and mix lightly with a fork. Cover and set aside to cool. The rice should be slightly warm so that the grains will stick together when rolling.

Place a bamboo sushi mat on a flat surface with the short edge nearest you. Cover the mat with 1 sheet of nori, scoop 1 cup of rice onto the nori and pat into an even layer all the way to the sides. (If rice sticks to your hands, dip them in water.) Leave a ½-inch border at the top and bottom edge of rice. Place one slice of the smoked fish across the bottom of the rice.

Using both hands, fold the bottom edge of the nori around the filling to form a "log," at the same time pushing the mat away from you. End with the seam side underneath. Squeeze gently to smooth out the roll. Remove mat and repeat the procedure with the remaining ingredients. You'll become more proficient with each of the six rolls.

Dip a sharp knife into water and even off the ends of each roll. Cut each one crosswise into eight even pieces, wiping and wetting the knife after each cut to help you cut cleanly.

Serve sushi pieces cut side up on a platter with some pickled ginger and wasabi on the side.

Makes six servings

Tom Yum Koong

This classic Thai soup is served at the Little Thai Market. Tak Lam, the owner who shared this recipe with us, said all ingredients are available from their stand. Galangal, also known as kalanta, is a popular Thai ingredient. It looks like ginger, but has a spicier flavor.

6 cups water
1 stalk lemon grass, lightly pounded
    and cut into 2-inch slices
3 lime leaves
3 slices galangal
1 tablespoon Tom yum spice paste
    (available in jars or bottles)
12 medium shrimp, shelled and
    deveined

10 mushrooms, thinly spliced
1 tablespoon salt
2 tablespoons fish sauce
3 tablespoons lime juice
6 hot peppers, pounded lightly
½ cup chopped coriander, for
    garnish

Bring water to a boil in a large saucepan. Add lemon grass, lime leaves, galangal and Tom yum paste. Cook for 2 to 3 minutes. Add all the shrimp and cook until lightly pink. Then add mushrooms and salt.

Remove pan from heat. Season with fish sauce, lime juice and hot peppers. Garnish with coriander and serve hot.

Makes four servings

Tommy DiNic's Pulled Pork

Tommy DiNic's has sold roast pork sandwiches for 60 years and, to this day, believes it's a wonderful sandwich. "A time came," added Joe Nicolosi, head chef and owner along with his father, "when we thought we could do even better, and push the pork envelope just a bit further." So sometime in 2007, they experimented with making a pulled pork sandwich, a non-BBQ variety. It maintains the flavor of the roast pork, but in a richer, fuller form. Pulled pork quickly became the second biggest seller next to their legendary roast pork sandwich. Given time, it may even be first!

1 pork shoulder butt, about
   9 pounds

DRY RUB
3 teaspoons kosher salt
1 teaspoon oregano
1 teaspoon thyme
1 teaspoon black pepper
2 teaspoons granulated garlic
2 teaspoons granulated fennel
¼ teaspoon hot pepper flakes

1 sprig fresh rosemary
6 garlic cloves, minced
1 Spanish onion, chopped
1 6-inch-square pig skin
½ cup dry red wine
Water or a combination of
   homemade stock and water

Trim excess fat off pork butt, cut open above bone and leave bone in.

To make dry rub, combine salt, oregano, thyme, pepper, granulated garlic, granulated fennel and hot pepper flakes.

Spread one-third of dry rub inside pork. Take rosemary off stem and add to inside of pork along with half of the minced garlic. Close meat and tie with butcher twine. Add another one-third of dry rub on top of pork butt. Add remaining third of dry rub on bottom of pork butt.

Preheat oven to 400 degrees.

Place pork in a large pan, fat side down. Cook for 45 minutes. Remove pan from oven, take meat out of pan and scrape bottom. Add chopped onion and remaining minced garlic to pan. Place the square of pork skin on top of onion mixture. Put pork butt back in pan, fat side up, and return to oven. Cook another 20 minutes.

Add red wine and cook another 15 minutes. Remove from oven and turn meat fat side down. Add enough water or a combination of stock and water to come halfway up side of pork. Return to oven and cook 30 minutes. At end of 30 minutes, cover pan tightly with aluminum foil. Reduce oven temperature to 250 degrees and cook an additional 4 hours. Remove from oven and discard pork skin.

Pour stock along with onion mixture from pan into a blender and blend until smooth. Place pork on cutting board, remove string and coarsely chop meat. Discard bone. Ladle gravy over pork and serve, or make sandwiches with pork and drizzle gravy on top.

Makes eight to 10 servings or 10 sandwiches

Joe and Tommy Nicolosi, proprietors of Tommy DiNic's,
famous for their roast pork, beef and veal sandwiches.

Turkey Diablo Hoagie

In addition to this Turkey Diablo Hoagie, the Chicken à la Rocco sandwich with sharp provolone and spicy Dijonnaise sauce is also popular at Carmen's Famous Hoagies and Cheesesteaks, along with their Special Italian Hoagie. The Turkey Diablo Hoagie was recently featured in *The Philadelphia Inquirer* as one of the 10 best hoagies in the Market. Carmen's famous Dijonnaise sauce can be purchased from their restaurant on a request-only basis. Here is their fabulous recipe.

 1 10-inch hoagie roll
 Carmen's Dijonnaise sauce to taste
 3 slices hot pepper cheese

 8 to 10 slices roast turkey breast
 Roasted sweet or hot peppers as
  desired

Slice open hoagie roll. Spread with Dijonnaise sauce. Add hot pepper cheese and pile on turkey breast. Top with roasted sweet or hot peppers. Serve.

Makes one hoagie

———

The neon sign at Carmen's.

Turkey Noodle Soup

The Original Turkey stand in the Market always draws a crowd. People love to watch the huge turkey breasts being expertly sliced down for platters and stacked high in sandwiches. This soup from The Original Turkey, owned by Roger Bassett, makes excellent use of cooked turkey meat.

3 quarts turkey or chicken stock
2 celery ribs, diced
1 large onion, diced
2 carrots, diced
½ cup chopped parsley
2 cups chopped tomatoes

1 tablespoon "crazy salt" (see Note below)
1 teaspoon basil
½ pound noodles
¾ pound cooked turkey, cut into chunks

Place stock in a large pot. Add celery, onion, carrot, parsley, tomato, "crazy salt" and basil. Bring to a slow boil, reduce heat and simmer for 1 hour. Add noodles and turkey chunks, stirring lightly. Let simmer 15 minutes, stirring occasionally, until noodles are done and turkey is heated through.

Makes eight servings

Note: The "crazy salt" used in this recipe is a blend of salt, marjoram and oregano.

Vegetable Lasagna with Tomato Cream Sauce

Preparing lasagna can be time-consuming, but using fresh pasta sheets, which don't need to be precooked, cuts down on preparation time, says George Mickel, owner of By George Pizza, Pasta & Cheesesteaks. In addition to prepared food, By George carries their own sauces and fresh pasta, cut or in sheets, as used in this recipe.

VEGETABLE MIXTURE

2 cups broccoli rabe

4 tablespoons olive oil

1 tablespoon sugar

1 onion, sliced

1 eggplant, peeled and sliced

2 red bell peppers

2 cups fresh spinach

2 cups fresh tomatoes, chopped

2 cups fresh mushrooms, chopped

RICOTTA MIXTURE

3 pounds ricotta cheese

1 tablespoon chopped parsley

1 tablespoon olive oil

1 tablespoon chopped fresh garlic

½ teaspoon salt and pepper

1 teaspoon grated pecorino Romano

TOMATO CREAM SAUCE

4 cups prepared marinara sauce

2 cups light cream

1 pound fresh egg pasta sheets

2 cups fresh mozzarella, sliced

Preheat oven to 375 degrees.

To prepare vegetables, cook broccoli rabe in boiling water for 4 minutes. Place in ice water for a few minutes, then drain and chop. In a skillet, add 2 tablespoons of the olive oil and sugar. Add sliced onions and cook about 10 to 15 minutes until caramelized. Set aside. In another skillet, heat the remaining olive oil and pan-fry eggplant until lightly browned. Season with salt and pepper to taste and set aside. Rub red peppers with a little olive oil and roast in oven until soft, about 10 to 15 minutes, then cool and slice. Combine all vegetables including spinach, tomatoes and mushrooms.

To make ricotta mixture, in a bowl, mix together the ricotta, parsley, oil, garlic, salt and pepper, and the grated cheese. Set aside.

To make tomato cream sauce, in a bowl, mix together marinara sauce and cream. Set aside.

In a 13 × 9-inch pan, spread tomato cream sauce (about ¼ inch up sides of pan). Place one layer of fresh pasta over sauce. Spread about ½ inch of ricotta mixture over pasta, and then add a layer of the vegetable mixture and more sauce. Add another layer of pasta and repeat layering until all ingredients are used. End with a layer of pasta topped with tomato cream sauce. Cover with foil and bake for 70 minutes. Take out pan, top with fresh mozzarella cheese and cook, uncovered, until cheese is melted. Remove from oven and allow lasagna to sit for 15 minutes before serving (this will help to hold it together).

Serves eight to 10 people

By George Pizza, Pasta and Cheesesteaks.

Vegetarian Chili

This chili recipe came from Jill Horn, who once owned Vorspeise. Her shop was a part of the Market for many years, and this recipe was part of the original *Reading Terminal Market Cookbook*. It is an example of the healthy foods Jill served to her customers.

1 tablespoon olive oil
2 cups diced onions
1 cup diced carrots
4 garlic cloves, minced
1 tablespoon chili powder
2 teaspoons ground cumin
1 teaspoon ground coriander
1 teaspoon ground cinnamon
¼ teaspoon cayenne pepper
Freshly ground black pepper to taste
1 28-ounce can Italian plum tomatoes

1 can water, from empty tomato can
¼ cup wheat berries
¼ cup lentils
2 15-ounce cans kidney beans, or ½
    pound dried (see Note below)
1 15-ounce can navy or great
    northern beans, or ¼ pound
    dried (see Note below)
1 15-ounce can black beans, or ¼
    pound dried (see Note below)
½ cup bulgur wheat

In a large saucepan over low heat, heat oil and gently sauté the onions, carrots and garlic for 10 minutes, or until softened. Add chili powder, cumin, coriander, cinnamon, cayenne and black pepper and simmer for about 5 minutes, stirring frequently.

Add the tomatoes plus the can of water. Roughly break up the tomatoes with a wooden spoon. Add the wheat berries and simmer for ½ hour. Add the lentils and simmer another ½ hour, or until lentils and wheat berries are tender. Add more water if liquid reduces too much. The mixture should be soupy rather than like a stew. Add the cooked beans and the bulgur wheat. Stir gently over medium heat until bulgur has softened, about 5 to 6 minutes.

Makes six to eight servings

Note: To prepare dried beans, place them in a saucepan, cover with water and bring to a boil. Remove the pan from the heat, and let the beans sit in the water for 1 hour. Drain and rinse thoroughly. Cook beans in fresh water to cover for 1 hour, or until soft, then proceed with the recipe.

Wurstsalat

The following is a variation of a simple recipe for a popular German Brauhaus lunch presented by Wursthaus Schmitz. Sliced cold cuts are tossed in herb vinaigrette and served over a salad of lettuce, tomato, cucumber and red onion. It's a perfect summer dish enjoyed with a nice crisp glass of Riesling or a light pilsner. If Bierschinken or Lyoner are unavailable, you can substitute your favorite cold cuts.

HERB VINAIGRETTE

1 tablespoon Hengstenberg seasoned vinegar, or apple cider vinegar

1 tablespoon Thomy spicy German mustard

2 packets of Knorr brand Salad Kronung

½ cup cold water

½ cup canola oil

Salt and pepper, optional

SALAD FIXINGS

½ pound Bierschinken, sliced thin

½ pound Lyoner, sliced thin

1 tomato, sliced

1 cucumber, sliced

1 red onion, peeled and sliced

Salt and pepper, optional

1 small head of Boston Bibb lettuce, washed, leaves separated

To make herb vinaigrette, in a small bowl, mix together the vinegar, mustard, salad herbs (Salad Kronung) and water. Whisk in the oil until thoroughly combined. Season with salt and pepper, if desired.

In a large mixing bowl, arrange the cold cuts and pour the vinaigrette over the slices. Mix thoroughly. Let marinate for 30 minutes.

In another bowl, combine tomato, cucumber, red onion, plus salt and pepper, if desired.

To make salad, place lettuce on plates, top with tomato, cucumber and onion mixture, and then with marinated cold cuts. Serve immediately.

Makes four servings

Yu Shin Vegetable

Soon Ae Mun, owner of the Golden Bowl, told us that they still serve this vegetable dish and many others that the previous owner, Ms. Maw, gave to them. Ms. Maw's son David did most of the cooking, and he was emphatic about the use of some of the ingredients in this dish. Soon Ae Mun continues to use the same ingredients such as Chinese cooking sherry and light soy sauce, which is less salty than regular. The use of Worcestershire sauce in the recipe is a key addition. Serve this dish with rice.

SAUCE
1 cup chicken broth
½ cup dark sesame oil
¼ cup Chinese cooking sherry
1 teaspoon freshly grated ginger
1 teaspoon dried garlic or 2 garlic
 cloves, minced
1 teaspoon Worcestershire sauce
2 tablespoons oyster sauce
1 teaspoon hot pepper oil
2 tablespoons sugar
¼ cup light soy sauce
2 tablespoons vegetable oil
2 garlic cloves, minced

2 tablespoons vegetable oil
Florets from 1 bunch broccoli
2 carrots, thinly sliced
¼ pound mushrooms, thinly sliced
1 rib celery, thinly sliced
½ cup sliced water chestnuts
6 to 8 dried Chinese mushrooms,
 softened in hot water for 10
 minutes and drained
1 tablespoon cornstarch

In a bowl, combine chicken broth, sesame oil, sherry, ginger, half the garlic, Worcestershire sauce, half the oyster sauce, hot pepper oil, sugar and soy sauce. Set aside.

Heat a large skillet or wok and add vegetable oil. Add remaining garlic and remaining oyster sauce, mix well. Then add broccoli, carrots, mushrooms, celery, water chestnuts and Chinese mushrooms. Stir-fry for 2 to 3 minutes. Pour the sauce into the wok. When the sauce is boiling, sift in cornstarch, lower heat and cook until slightly thickened.

Makes four servings

Specialty Merchants and Market Services

EADING TERMINAL MARKET is home to many specialty shops. Some sell food, related grocery items and gift baskets, while others sell distinctive and interesting cooking supplies, cookbooks, new and used books, French linens, candles, flowers, clothing, crafts and jewelry made by local artisans. The Market has a demonstration kitchen, catering company and community room for special events, and even a shoeshine stand. All these merchants have and continue to play a special role in the Market and serve it well, creating a wonderful balance of exciting things to see and buy.

Flowers and Plants

As if Reading Terminal Market is not colorful enough, one is struck when entering from the 12th Street side by the burst of magnificent arrays of flowers at Market Blooms. Steve DeShong, owner of the shop, has been a part of the Market for more than 10 years. He has incredibly beautiful arrangements of fresh flowers from around the world and sensational seasonal selections. Steve owns a five-acre farm overflowing with plantings for all seasons. In addition, the shop carries a variety of vegetable and herb seeds year round, a third of which are organic. Top sellers are arugula, spinach, kale, collards and basil. Tomato seeds include beefsteak, Brandywine and heirloom.

Housewares, Books, Crafts, Etc.

Kitchen supply shops are a natural for Reading Terminal Market, and if you enter from the Arch Street side, that is one of the first things you'll see. Amy's Place opened in October 1994, and is owned by Amy Podolsky. The shop started as a 10 × 30-foot stall in the Market, selling tableware, linens, gifts and, most notably, aprons. "Finding my shop back then," she says, "was as easy as asking for the apron lady." In November 2007, Amy's Place relocated to a glass-enclosed space, doubling its size. The expansion allowed for significant growth. Today, she offers a wide selection of kitchen tools and gadgets, bakeware, cookie cutters, handcrafted serving pieces, textiles and a section devoted to cooking-related merchandise for children. Amy's Place is the quintessential shop for unique gift items for home

Jill Ross, proprietor of The Cookbook Stall, offering a wide range of works on the cooking arts.

chefs of all ages. Featured as "Store of the Month" by *Gourmet Insider* in August 2010, it's a great place to browse for the perfect gift or that kitchen tool you haven't been able to find anywhere else.

Contessa's French Linens is owned and operated by Laura DiFrancesco and is the only authentic French linen shop in Philadelphia. Laura, who entertains extensively, was often complimented on her French table linens. After many years, she decided to open her own shop. Laura flew to France, searched out the merchandise she wanted to present and opened in the Market six years ago. The shop offers a wide selection of linens from Provence and Brittany in France and from other European countries, as well as traditional, handmade Moroccan-French market baskets. Laura carries cloth table linens in beautiful patterns, laminated tablecloths, Quimper porcelain from Brittany, authentic Polish stoneware, jewelry, purses, scarves and Provençal dresses for little girls that are actually made from tablecloth material from the south of France.

The Cookbook Stall is another natural for the Market. Currently run by Jill Ross, it is an independent, woman-owned bookshop that has been in place for over 20 years. It was named fifth in the world for cookbooks and for books on culinary adventures and interesting kitchen items by *Saveur* magazine. The store offers books ranging from sous vide, knife skills and sushi-rolling to making cupcakes, baby food and dog biscuits. There is something here for everyone, from professional chefs to those just learning to boil water. The Cookbook Stall continues to assist those who love to cook in finding recipes for every taste.

City Kitchen at the Reading Terminal Market is a state-of-the-art facility used for a variety of cooking classes and private culinary events. Prominent Philadelphia chefs and other members of the food community are showcased, as well as Market merchants featuring their signature foods.

A stroll around the Market will bring you to other interesting stalls that have no connection to food. Miscellaneous Libri, a stand concentrating on new and used books covering an immense range of subjects, is one of the most popular. The original owner is still there, and his customers come from all over the world.

Other nonfood merchants selling crafts, clothing and items for the discerning shopper include Amazulu, owned by designer Charita Powell, featuring handcrafted jewelry, wearable art and unusual home décor items—some made locally, others from distant places. Market customers love to browse and buy a piece or more from the collection of earrings, bracelets and necklaces crafted by talented artisans.

At the De Village booth, Joycelyn and Watson Parks bring African art to the Market, as well as ladies' and men's apparel, jewelry and accessories—a browser's paradise within a busy farmer's market. The shop, which has been at Reading Terminal for over 15 years, not only attracts tourists and conventioneers looking for locally made items, but also is frequented by everyday shoppers looking for something a little bit different for themselves.

Terralyn Bath, Body, Spirit, owned by Lynette Manteau, specializes in handmade, vegetable-based soaps, all-natural skin care products, lotions and therapeutic bath salts. Her homemade items are manufactured less than a mile from the Market. Lynette, an avid customer, was hired as an administrative assistant. She presented her idea and a sampling of her soaps to the Market's general manager, and the rest is history. After starting with a small cart in 2002, she now has a stand brimming with products. Lynette says her best-sellers are lemongrass and loofah soap, coconut bath salt, lemonade shampoo, and "Take a Hike" all-natural insect repellent.

Finally, the famous Shoe Doctor has been a part of the Market for over 21 years. Philadelphians, tourists and celebrities stop by to chat and have their shoes shined. Some of our sources have worked at the Market for many years and have interesting stories to tell, but other stories will stay at the Shoe Doctor's. We were told that the biggest tip received from a popular talk show host was a hundred dollar bill.

Specialty Foods

Where else but in Reading Terminal Market does one get such a strong feeling for Philadelphia as a melting pot? The ethnic diversity of the specialty food merchants is well reflected in this special place. You can take advantage of a vast assemblage of international foods and eclectic products, all available under one roof. Each has its own character and personality.

Bee Natural specializes, as its name implies, in all things bee-related and naturally produced. Darren Sausser, its owner for more than a decade, starting keeping bees while living on a farm in New York, where he started by selling beeswax candles; he continued his passion when he moved to a farm in Delaware. The counter of his stand in the Market is lined with jar after jar, large and small, of a wide selection of honeys. According to the staff, the most popular are the Butter Bean Bee Natural Honey and the raw honey. Also available is Chunk Pure Honey with Comb. The shelves are full of handmade beeswax candles and products. The

Chocolate by Mueller.

candles are all-natural and smokeless. Bee Natural is a great place to pick a special gift for someone or just to treat yourself to some natural relaxation.

Glen and Theresa Mueller have captured a child's (and an adult's) dream of candy heaven with their old-time candy store, Chocolate by Mueller, which has been in the Market for over 20 years. Remember licorice twizzlers, hand-dipped chocolate marshmallow pops, colorful marzipan, chocolates filled with luscious creams and decadent truffles? They're all here in row after row. In addition to more traditional chocolates and confections are some not-so-ordinary ones, like solid chocolate molded into anatomically correct hearts, lungs, noses, kidneys, livers and brains with a tag that reads, "You're always on my mind." These were thought up by Theresa during one of her very infrequent quiet times. She was featured in *Ripley's Believe It or Not,* and the shop was included on the TV show, *Bizarre Foods.* Glen Mueller Jr., their son, has his own stand nearby. The younger Glen admits he had no intention of joining the family business, but after the military, he was persuaded by his father to help him in the Market, and the rest is history. Glen's shop has been there for 16 years. He makes chocolate seven days a week and features a variety of chocolate-covered pretzels and, not to be outdone by his parents, chocolate-covered onions. In addition, he sells caramel candy apples, chocolate-covered strawberries when available, sea salt caramel pretzels and his best-seller, the unique peanutzel—a pretzel coated in peanut butter chocolate, then coated with milk or dark chocolate.

Herbiary is a serene herbal shop owned by a husband and wife, Andrew Celwyn and Maria Toll. The Market location is their second store and opened in 2010. They specialize in chemical-free, all-natural products such as organic plant medicine, tinctures, dietary supplements, teas, extracts, essential oils, and even natural bug-repellent candles. The staff is friendly and knowledgeable about all their products and takes the time to help customers find just what they're looking for.

Jonathan Best Gourmet Grocer is a true food emporium with an extensive, eclectic mix of merchandise. David Scheiber, who named the grocery after his oldest son, specializes in carrying domestic and imported groceries and cooking ingredients, including many hard-to-find food items. David is more than happy to search for and order an ingredient a customer can't find anywhere else. In addition to raw ingredients, you can purchase soups, vegan sandwiches, panini, wraps and freshly made salad boxes. Make sure to try one of their store-made fresh lemonades and teas, including ginger, blueberry and raspberry.

The sign above the Herbiary.

Pennsylvania General Store opened in the Market in 1987. Michael and Julie Holahan conceived the store as a source for Pennsylvania-made foods and crafts. They created a country-style general store whose shelves are filled with such familiar names as chocolate Wilbur Buds, Cope's Dried Sweet Corn, Bauman's Apple Butter, Burnt Cabin Pancake Mix and Asher's chocolate-covered pretzels and potato chips—piled high to tempt those who walk by. On the shelves you'll find jugs of locally produced Pennsylvania maple syrup, and displayed around the shop are many colorful Amish quilts and ceramics. Gift baskets of Pennsylvania products are mailed nationwide, and the store's catalogue abounds with ideas. The Pennsylvania General Store is the quintessential shopping place for Philadelphia and Keystone State items.

The Head Nut, a popular addition to the Market, sells an excellent variety of nuts, including wasabi almonds and buffalo peanuts—all ready to be scooped up, weighed and enjoyed. But the Head Nut offers so much more. There you can find vanilla sugar, gluten-free tapioca flour, sweet cream buttermilk powder, smoked chili powder and chipotle powder. A variety of curry powders and a selection of herbs are in stock. Coffee beans and teas may be purchased loose, including pomegranate green tea and black mint apricot tea. Also available are dried fruits, beans and grains. Here you can locate unusual ingredients that can't be found anywhere else.

The Tubby Olive is a tasting emporium owned by Nancy Murray and Sharon Huss. They are known for their wide selection of traditional, infused and organic olive oils, as well as white and dark balsamic vinegars. Their traditional oils come from California, Chile, Australia, Tunisia and Sicily. Flavored oils include blood orange, chipotle, Persian lime and harissa. Apricot, dark chocolate, espresso, fig, pomegranate, tangerine and violet are but a few of their interesting and unusual balsamic vinegars. Tasting before buying is fun, and the store's customer service experts can help guide you to just the right flavor combinations and can assist you in choosing custom gifts for special occasions. In addition to the Market, The Tubby Olive has a store in nearby Newtown Square.

Market Services

The Reading Terminal Market Merchants' Catering Company has many onsite events, both large and small. They have catered corporate events, weddings, rehearsal dinners and bar mitzvahs for groups ranging from 100 to 2000 people.

These functions are managed by Sarah Morrison of All About Events. Sarah has been a wedding and event planner for nearly a decade. One of her most memorable projects was planning a wedding held at the Market for the daughter of one of its own merchants. Sarah remembers coming to the Market as a youngster and adds, "I love that I am now actually working here." A common thread throughout this book is the love and dedication of everyone involved in the Market family.

Past Merchants of the Market

Margerum's Old Fashion (that was the spelling) Corner was one of the oldest businesses in Reading Terminal Market. It is a true part of the history of the Market and, at one time, occupied about a quarter of its space. William B. Margerum opened the store in 1902 and, with a fleet of cars, would deliver to customers outside Philadelphia. When the store first opened, it offered a variety of products, including poultry, meat and butter. Noelle Margerum took over the business in 1970 and stayed until its closing in 2012, representing the fourth generation of her family to run the operation. The store became more specialized, the shelves packed with a variety of canned, bottled and dried goods, beans and grains that were displayed in replicas of the original bins.

Nancy Marcus was the original owner of The Cookbook Stall, along with her husband, Ed. After publishing her own cookbook, she was actively involved in the subject, leading to the idea of opening her own cookbook store. In 1983, her dream was realized. The Cookbook Stall remains at the Market, although it was sold in 2003 to Jill Ross, the current owner.

The Spice Terminal was a Market staple from 1981 until its closing after the death of its longtime proprietor, Al Starzi. It was a well-stocked shop, filled nearly to the roof with everything that the store's name would suggest.

Although some of these stores are no longer in the Market or are under new ownership, we have kept their recipes in this new edition of *The Reading Terminal Market Cookbook*.

Apple Butter Spread

Traditionally, apple and other fruit butters were made in large copper kettles. The process took a whole day, with everyone stirring until the fruit formed a butter-like consistency. The Pennsylvania General Store carries a wide variety of fruit butters. This spread is delicious on muffins, scones, cornbread, toast or bagels, and it's great on pancakes.

    1 10-ounce jar apple butter
    6 ounces cream cheese, softened

Place the apple butter and cream cheese in a food processor or blender and process until smooth. Serve at room temperature. Refrigerate any leftover spread.

Makes one cup

*Michael and Julie Holahan, proprietors of
The Pennsylvania General Store, specializing in
Pennsylvania-made foods, crafts and gift baskets.*

Best Brown Bread Recipe

This recipe is from Laura DiFrancesco, owner of Contessa's French Linens. It yields a quick and easy, no-yeast, traditional brown bread. Laura loves to cook for family and friends, and she serves this bread alongside Irish stew on cold, wintry days.

Shortening for greasing pan

1 cup all-purpose flour
1 cup whole wheat flour
½ cup steel-cut oats (Scottish or Irish oatmeal)
½ cup cornmeal

½ cup rye four
1 teaspoon baking soda
1 teaspoon baking powder
1 teaspoon salt
1 egg, organic
2 cups buttermilk
¼ cup molasses

Preheat oven to 325 degrees.

Grease a 9 × 5-inch loaf pan.

In a large bowl, combine first eight ingredients. Set aside.

In another bowl, whisk egg, buttermilk and molasses. Gently stir egg mixture into dry ingredients until moistened. Do not over-mix.

Pour batter into prepared pan and bake for approximately 45 to 50 minutes, or until a toothpick inserted in center comes out clean.

Cool for 10 minutes before removing from pan to a wire rack. Cool completely. Serve.

Makes one loaf

Black Bean Pot

Dried beans have always been available at the Market. Many of the current specialty merchants carry a wide selection. This heartwarming winter bean dish comes from Noelle Margerum, who owned Margerum's Old Fashion Corner, once an important part of the Market. It freezes well, so make it in large batches. Black beans, sometimes called turtle beans, are oval with black skins and are rich in taste. In addition to going well in soups and stews, they are a colorful addition to vegetable salads. Pinto beans are medium-sized with beige and brown speckles and are popular in many Mexican and Tex-Mex dishes. Kidney beans are red or white. The white ones are sometimes called cannellini beans. The red beans are most often used in chili, while the white beans are popular in Italian dishes.

½ pound dried black beans	2 bay leaves
¼ pound dried pinto beans	1 teaspoon salt
¼ pound dried kidney beans	2 tablespoons molasses
3 tablespoons olive oil	2 tablespoons honey
1 small onion, chopped	¼ cup packed brown sugar
2 garlic cloves, minced	¼ cup dark rum
1 rib celery, chopped	2 teaspoons dry mustard
1 carrot, chopped	1 teaspoon dried thyme
6 cups water	2 tablespoons butter or margarine

Rinse beans thoroughly, sorting through and removing any debris. Place beans in a large saucepan, add water to cover and let sit for 2 to 3 hours. Drain. Return beans to saucepan and set aside.

In a medium skillet, heat oil, then add onion, garlic, celery and carrot. Cook until onion is tender, but not browned, about 2 minutes. Transfer mixture into the beans, and add the water, bay leaves and salt. Place saucepan over medium heat and bring to a boil. Reduce heat, cover and simmer until beans are almost tender, about 1½ hours. During cooking, add more hot water as needed to keep beans covered.

Drain beans, reserving cooking liquid. Remove bay leaves.

Preheat oven to 300 degrees.

In a bowl, combine molasses, honey, brown sugar, 2 tablespoons of the rum, dry mustard and thyme. Mix well.

Place beans in an ovenproof casserole and stir in the molasses mixture. Add enough reserved cooking liquid to just cover beans. Cover pan and bake for 1 hour. Uncover, dot with butter or margarine, and bake for an additional 20 minutes. Stir in remaining rum just before serving.

Makes six to eight servings

Bob's Onion Dip

This recipe is from Sarah Morrison of All About Events, the catering company that handles special events at the Reading Terminal Market. A family favorite created by her grandfather, she fondly remembers it being served at every family function. "We fought over the last drop," she recalls. Serve in a glass or ceramic bowl with potato chips, hard pretzels or your favorite crackers.

3 8-ounce packages cream cheese   ⅛ to ¼ cup milk
1 large onion, finely grated

Combine cream cheese and onion in the bowl of a mixer. Blend together, adding enough milk to reach dipping consistency. Chill before serving.

Makes 6 to 8 servings

Chicken Braised in Vinegar

For many years, Leonard Podagrosi managed The Spice Terminal, once the go-to place in the Market for spices and much more. Although The Spice Terminal is no longer a part of the Market, we have kept this recipe from our first *Reading Terminal Market Cookbook.* This is one of Leonard's favorite dishes, given to him by his mother. It uses no oil or salt.

1 whole chicken, about 3½ pounds, cut into serving pieces and skinned

2 teaspoons ground rosemary

2 teaspoons garlic powder

1 teaspoon paprika

Freshly ground black pepper to taste

4 bay leaves

1½ cups red wine vinegar

Preheat oven to 350 degrees.

Place chicken pieces in a baking dish, season with rosemary, garlic powder, paprika and black pepper. Place bay leaves on top. Bake approximately 10 minutes, or until spices are nicely browned. Pour vinegar on top and cook for about 1 hour, or until the liquid has turned into a glaze and chicken is done. Remove bay leaves and serve.

Makes four servings

Chicken with Raspberry Shrub

A shrub is a mixture of fruit juice, vinegar, sugar, honey, maple syrup and spices. It has an intense flavor that livens up a variety of dishes, and it was used in many drinks during Colonial times. This recipe comes from Julie and Michael Holahan, owners of the Pennsylvania General Store. Shrub mixtures are available there.

Flour for dredging	2 tablespoons olive oil
4 chicken cutlets, cut into thin strips	2 celery ribs, thinly sliced
2 tablespoons butter	¼ cup raspberry shrub
	Freshly ground pepper to taste

Lightly flour the chicken strips, shaking off excess flour. In a medium skillet, heat butter and oil together until hot. Brown chicken strips quickly on both sides, 2 to 3 minutes total. Remove chicken from skillet and set aside.

If necessary, add a little more butter or oil to skillet. Add celery and stir-fry for 1 to 2 minutes. Return chicken to skillet, add the shrub, season with black pepper and cook for another 1 to 2 minutes, or until shrub lightly glazes the chicken.

Makes four servings

Chili

Amy Podolsky from Amy's Place likes to prepare this version of chili for gatherings of friends during the cold winter months. Not only are all the ingredients for this recipe available at the Market, but at Amy's Place you can also find the perfect bowls to serve it in.

½ cup olive oil
1 large onion, coarsely chopped
1 pound sweet Italian sausage, removed from casing
1 pound ground beef
2 tablespoons tomato paste
3 garlic cloves, minced
2 teaspoons ground cumin
2 tablespoons chili powder
1 tablespoon Dijon mustard

2 teaspoons dried oregano
1 teaspoon salt
1 teaspoon black pepper
1 28-ounce can Italian plum tomatoes
⅓ cup red wine
½ cup chopped flat-leaf parsley
1 15-ounce can kidney beans
1 cup pitted black olives

In a large saucepan, heat oil over low heat. Add onion and cook, covered, until soft and translucent, 5 to 8 minutes. Break the sausage meat and ground beef into the saucepan and cook over medium heat until well browned. Drain any excess fat.

Stir in tomato paste, garlic, cumin, chili powder, mustard, oregano, salt and pepper. Add the tomato, wine, parsley and drained beans. Stir well and simmer, uncovered, about 30 minutes. Taste for seasoning. Add olives and simmer an additional 5 minutes. Serve.

Makes six to eight servings

Conley's Irish Scone

Laura DiFrancesco of Contessa's French Linens shared this recipe with us. Laura, a former culinary instructor, has won numerous recipe contests and has appeared on PBS Channel 12. She says this scone recipe freezes very well and makes for excellent gift-giving at holiday time.

Shortening for greasing pans
4 cups all-purpose flour, sifted
¾ cup sugar
4 teaspoons baking powder
½ teaspoon baking soda

1 teaspoon salt
1 cup dark raisins, soaked in hot
   water for 5 minutes
2 eggs
2 cups buttermilk

Preheat oven to 350 degrees.

Grease two 9 × 5-inch loaf pans (a large tube pan may be used; increase cooking time to 1 hour).

In a large bowl, combine flour, sugar, baking powder, baking soda and salt. Drain raisins and add to mixture.

In another bowl, blend eggs and buttermilk. Gently fold egg/buttermilk mixture into the dry ingredients.

Pour batter into prepared pans and bake for 35 to 40 minutes, or until lightly browned.

Makes two loaves

Garlic and Ginger Hummus

This garlic and ginger hummus is from David Scheiber, owner of Jonathan Best Gourmet Grocer. The ginger in the recipe adds a special kick. This wonderful version is made without tahini, a high-fat ingredient found in most other hummus recipes.

3 tablespoons lemon juice
1 teaspoon chopped fresh ginger
2 garlic cloves, sliced in half
½ teaspoon cumin, or to taste

1 15-ounce can chickpeas, drained
  and rinsed
⅓ cup olive oil, more if needed
Salt and pepper to taste

In the bowl of a food processor fitted with a metal blade, blend together lemon juice, ginger, garlic and cumin. Add chickpeas and puree. With machine running, add olive oil in a steady stream and process until smooth and creamy. Add more oil if needed to reach desired consistency. Blend in salt and pepper to taste. Serve.

Makes about 1½ cups

Honorary Contributor: Rick Nichols

The Rick Nichols Room in the Market honors Rick Nichols, who for years was a journalist for *The Philadelphia Inquirer* and covered restaurants and food trends throughout the Philadelphia area. His belief in the importance of the Market, not only to the city, but to all the people who visited made him a strong proponent. Rick did all he could to keep this special place alive and vital. It seemed only fitting that a community room be set aside for hosting Market events and those intended for the general public. Since its opening, The Rick Nichols Room has hosted gatherings including tastings, corporate meetings, private parties, book signings and numerous other special events. When not in use, it's a nice spot to sit and relax. Covering the walls of the room is a plethora of fascinating information to read about the Market.

Paprikash à la Szokan

"That soulful paprikash is the one we revert to, time and again, our comfort food of first resort; to blunt raw winter nights and feed sudden gusts of hungry friends."

—Rick Nichols

This succulent, fall-off-the-bone chicken recipe was submitted by Rick Nichols. The community room bears his name for all his efforts in helping the Market over the years. The credit for this recipe, as he will attest, goes to his wife Nancy and her family, who are half Slovak and half Hungarian-Romanian. Fortunately, Nancy had asked her mother, Helen Szokan, to write down her recipes, and we are so grateful she did. It requires only five main ingredients and little else to make it a full meal. Add a simple cucumber salad, and make sure to have lots of bread for the delicious gravy.

3 to 4 tablespoons vegetable or canola oil
1 large onion, chopped
2 tablespoons sweet paprika
Salt and pepper to taste

1 chicken fryer, 3 pounds or more, cut in serving pieces
½ pint (1 cup) sour cream
1 to 2 tablespoons all-purpose flour or more if needed

In a deep-sided frying pan or large pot, heat oil. Cook onions until translucent. Stir in paprika.

Salt and pepper the chicken on both sides and add pieces to pan, skin side down. Brown for about 2 minutes, then turn over, coating chicken with the sauce. Cover and cook over low heat, turning chicken every 15 minutes for about an hour, or until the meat is almost falling off the bone. If it seems to be drying out, add up to ¼ cup of water. After the first 45 minutes, take off the lid. Turn off heat. Remove chicken and place in a bowl, discarding skin. Keep warm.

Add sour cream to the pan juices, then whisk in some flour as needed to thicken sauce.

Turn heat back on, add chicken parts with any juices accumulated in bowl and reheat gently for about 5 minutes.

Makes four servings

James' Truffle Dip

For everyone from the novice cook to the seasoned chef, The Tubby Olive has a multitude of inspiring oil and vinegar flavors as well as recipe ideas to please your palate and fit your culinary needs. This recipe is sure to do just that and will be a success at your next party. The staff suggests serving the dip with kettle-style chips or pretzel sticks.

½ cup Greek yogurt
½ cup sour cream
½ cup Gorgonzola or another blue cheese, crumbled
3 tablespoons black or white truffle oil

2 tablespoons minced fresh chives, plus more for garnish
1 tablespoon fresh lemon juice
½ teaspoon salt
½ teaspoon pepper or to taste

In a bowl, mix together yogurt and sour cream until incorporated. Add remaining ingredients and combine thoroughly. Refrigerate for a minimum of ½ hour for flavors to blend together. Garnish with chives.

Makes one cup

The sign at The Tubby Olive, offering olive oils and vinegars on tap.

Maple Syrup Quickbread

Maple syrup comes from the sap of the maple tree, and a good yield depends on the right combination of cool nights and warm days. At the beginning of spring, the syrup is quite clear, but it becomes darker and stronger-flavored as spring progresses. When the sap has been collected, it is boiled down, with 40 to 60 gallons of sap needed to produce a single gallon of syrup. Pennsylvania is the country's fourth largest syrup-producing state. This recipe, like the pure maple syrup it uses, comes from the Pennsylvania General Store.

¼ pound (1 stick) unsalted butter,
   softened
1 tablespoon sugar
2 large eggs, beaten
⅔ cup buttermilk
⅓ cup maple syrup
1 cup whole-wheat flour
1 cup all-purpose flour

1 teaspoon baking powder
½ teaspoon baking soda
½ teaspoon salt
1½ cups coarsely grated apple
   (about 2 apples)
½ cup crushed walnuts
Cream cheese for spreading

Preheat oven to 350 degrees.

Grease a 9 × 5-inch loaf pan and set aside.

In a large bowl, cream butter and sugar together, then beat in eggs. Add buttermilk and maple syrup and stir just until mixed. Into this mixture, sift the flours, baking powder, baking soda and salt. Stir until well combined. Add the apple and walnuts and mix gently. Spoon batter into prepared loaf pan and bake for 50 to 60 minutes, or until a cake tester inserted into center comes out clean. Turn bread out onto a rack and let cool completely. Slice and serve with cream cheese.

Makes one loaf

Market Customer: Anonymous

Saffron is one of the world's most expensive spices. Dried crocus-flower stigmas are hand-picked, but each blossom yields only three stigmas. Saffron gives a beautiful yellow color and a subtle flavor to rice and other dishes. It should be bought in threads, rather than ground, for a fresher flavor. Saffron is available at many of the grocery shops in the Market. Before using saffron, the threads are always steeped in a hot liquid to impart their color and flavor to the liquid. This recipe comes from a Market customer who wishes to remain anonymous.

Basmati Rice with Saffron

1 teaspoon saffron

3 tablespoons milk, warmed

2 cups basmati rice

2 tablespoons vegetable oil

3 cardamom pods

2 cinnamon sticks

4 cups water

¼ teaspoon salt

In a small bowl, soak the saffron in the warmed milk for 10 to 15 minutes. Wash the rice under cold water several times until water runs clear.

In a medium-size, heavy-bottomed saucepan, heat oil. Place the cardamom and cinnamon sticks in pan and stir a few times. Add the rice and toss together, making sure the rice is well coated with the oil.

Add water and salt, bring to a boil, cover, reduce heat to a simmer and cook for about 15 minutes. Pour in saffron liquid and toss lightly with a fork. Cover and cook another 10 minutes, or until rice is tender. Fluff rice with a fork and serve immediately.

Makes six servings

Market Customer: Sarah Oaks

Sarah Oaks has worked in Philadelphia for decades and has been a regular Reading Terminal Market customer for over 25 years. She says that "Everyone who tries this heirloom cake from my family's archives agrees it's the moistest and most delicious honey cake ever." In this recipe, Sarah likes to use the darker honey available from Bee Natural in the Market. According to her grandmother, the amounts of spices are only suggestions. You can adjust the quantities to suit your own taste.

Sarah's Grandmother's Holiday Honey Cake

COFFEE MIXTURE
1 teaspoon baking soda
8-ounce cup of very hot, double-
    strength coffee

½ cup raisins, optional
3 cups plus 1 tablespoon all-
    purpose flour
1 tablespoon baking powder
1 teaspoon ground cinnamon
½ teaspoon pumpkin pie spice

½ teaspoon powdered ginger
¼ teaspoon salt
1 cup granulated sugar
½ cup brown sugar
1 egg
½ cup vegetable oil
1 cup honey
½ cup chopped walnuts
Powdered sugar for dusting,
    optional

In a 2-cup glass measuring cup, stir baking soda into hot coffee. Set aside to cool. Mixture should foam.

Preheat oven to 350 degrees.

Thoroughly grease and flour a 10-cup Bundt pan. (This is very important to prevent cake from sticking to sides of pan.)

If using raisins, soak in one cup boiling water. Set aside.

In a bowl, sift flour, baking powder, cinnamon, pumpkin pie spice, powdered ginger and salt.

In a large mixing bowl, add granulated sugar, brown sugar and egg, then beat on medium speed with a stand or hand-held mixer until creamed. Add vegetable oil.

Add honey to the empty vegetable oil measuring cup (this will help it to slide out), then add to mixing bowl. Combine well. Set aside.

If using raisins, drain well and coat with flour. Add nuts to raisins, if desired. Set aside.

Add coffee mixture and flour mixture to mixing bowl in three additions, alternating coffee and flour. Scrape down sides of bowl often. Batter will be thin. Continue mixing just until flour is incorporated.

If using raisins and nuts, fold into batter.

Pour batter into prepared pan and bake in center of oven for 45 minutes. Do not open oven door during cooking. After 45 minutes, test cake by pressing on surface to see if it springs back. If not, bake in 5-minute increments until cake does spring back. It burns easily, so make sure to check often.

When cake is done, remove from oven and immediately turn cake out onto a cooling rack. Do not let cake cool in pan—it will stick to sides.

Dust with powdered sugar, if desired.

Makes 10 to 12 servings

Meatless Moussaka

This recipe is from Stormy Lundy, who for many years ran the Reading Terminal Market Merchants' Catering Company. She uses shiitake and crimini mushrooms in the filling, making it a wonderful meatless alternative to the traditional moussaka, made with ground beef.

3 medium eggplants
Salt
Flour for dredging
Olive oil and vegetable oil for frying

Salt and pepper to taste
3 egg whites, beaten until stiff
    (reserve egg yolks for béchamel)
6 tablespoons fine bread crumbs

FILLING

4 tablespoons (½ stick) butter
1 pound shiitake mushrooms, finely
    chopped
1 pound crimini mushrooms, finely
    chopped
1 large onion, minced
¼ cup parsley, minced
1½ teaspoons tomato paste
½ cup water
½ cup dry white wine

**BÉCHAMEL SAUCE WITH EGG
    YOLKS**

7 tablespoons butter
7 tablespoons all-purpose flour
4 cups whole milk, scalded
2 cups low fat milk, scalded
3 egg yolks, beaten
1 cup grated Kefalotiri cheese
    (Locatelli or Parmesan may be
    substituted)

Preheat oven to 350 degrees.

Slice eggplants ¼-inch thick, and place on a platter in a single layer. Sprinkle with salt on both sides. Let stand at least 10 minutes, or until liquid beads form on surfaces. Take each slice, squeeze well between both hands or press down with a heavy weight, being sure all liquid is squeezed out.

Dip each slice lightly in flour. Shake off excess. In a large skillet, heat olive oil and vegetable oil. Fry eggplant, turning once, until golden brown. Drain on paper towels. Set aside. (Add more olive oil and vegetable oil to skillet, as needed, to fry all eggplant slices.)

For filling, in a large skillet, melt butter. Add mushrooms and onion, and cook until golden. Add parsley, tomato paste, water, wine, salt and pepper. Cook until all liquid has evaporated, about 20 minutes. Cool.

Beat egg white until soft mounds form. Fold in half the bread crumbs. Fold egg-white mixture into mushroom mixture.

To make béchamel sauce, in a medium-size saucepan, melt butter. Stir in flour and cook for 4 minutes over low heat, stirring constantly. Do not brown. Pour in the warm milk slowly, then stir and cook over low heat until sauce thickens. Cool. Whisk in egg yolks.

To assemble, oil a 13 × 9 × 1½-inch baking pan. Dust with remaining bread crumbs. Place a single layer of eggplant on bottom of pan. Cover with mushroom mixture and layer the remaining eggplant on top. Sprinkle with cheese and top with béchamel sauce.

Bake for about 30 minutes, or until golden brown. Cool. Cut into squares and serve.

Makes 10 servings

Sun-Dried Tomato Torta

This tasty appetizer came from Noelle Margerum. The Margerums were one of the founding families of the Market. Although they no longer own a shop there, this recipe, from our first *Reading Terminal Market Cookbook,* is still a favorite. The torta is easily put together and can be made two or three days ahead. Serve with crackers or dark bread. Toss any leftovers on hot pasta. Sun-dried tomatoes can be bought already packed in oil, but if you want to make them yourself, cut plum tomatoes in half, place them on a baking tray, and roast in a 150- to 200-degree oven for 6 to 8 hours, or until they turn dark red and are shriveled slightly. They can then be preserved in olive oil.

8 ounces cream cheese
¼ pound (1 stick) unsalted butter, room temperature, cut in pieces
1 garlic clove, cut in large pieces
1 cup freshly grated Parmesan cheese

½ cup sun-dried tomatoes in oil, drained and chopped, oil reserved, plus 3 sun-dried tomatoes, thinly sliced for garnish
2 cups tightly packed fresh basil leaves for garnish

In a blender or food processor, mix cream cheese, butter, garlic and Parmesan cheese until smooth. Remove half the cheese mixture and place in a bowl. Add the ½ cup sun-dried tomatoes and 1 tablespoon of the reserved tomato oil to the remaining cheese mixture. Blend until smooth. Scrape the mixture into the reserved cheese and mix with a fork until blended. Cover and refrigerate 20 minutes, or until firm enough to shape.

On a platter, form the cheese mixture into a mound, smoothing it with a spatula. Cover with an inverted bowl (do not use plastic wrap because it will stick to cheese) and chill 2 to 3 hours. Remove bowl and bring cheese to room temperature. Arrange basil leaves around the cheese torta and garnish with sun-dried tomato slices.

Makes eight servings

Swiss Chard Dip

Swiss chard comes in two varieties, green and red, both of which have a similar taste. Trim off any tough ribs on large leaves, and chop them before using. This recipe comes from Nancy Marcus, who is best remembered in the Market as the original owner of The Cookbook Stall.

1 pound Swiss chard, use leaves only, rinse, dry and coarsely chop
1 large onion, finely chopped
1 garlic clove, minced

½ teaspoon dried red pepper flakes
⅓ cup olive oil
¼ teaspoon salt
Juice of ½ lemon
Pita bread, cut into wedges

In a large saucepan, combine the chard, onion, garlic, pepper flakes and olive oil. Cook covered over medium heat for about 20 minutes, stirring occasionally until leaves are wilted. Reduce heat and continue cooking, covered, for about 1 hour, stirring occasionally until chard mixture thickens.

Transfer to a serving bowl. Sprinkle with salt and lemon juice. Cool. Serve at room temperature with pita bread.

Makes six servings

Tomato Sauce

This basic tomato sauce can be at the heart of so many great meals: pizza, pasta dishes, sautéed vegetables and soups, just to name a few favorites. The sauce freezes beautifully, and you'll be one step closer to preparing a quick, easy and delicious meal. Best of all, these ingredients can be purchased from Jonathan Best Gourmet Grocer, who supplied us with this recipe.

¼ cup extra virgin olive oil
4 garlic cloves, minced
2 medium onions, diced
1½ teaspoons sea salt
¼ cup tomato paste
1 teaspoon dried oregano
½ cup red wine

2 tablespoons red wine vinegar
2 28-ounce cans whole peeled tomatoes with juice (cut tomatoes in half, squeeze to remove seeds)
½ cup chopped fresh basil
Freshly ground pepper to taste

In a Dutch oven, heat oil over medium heat. Add garlic and cook, stirring constantly, until fragrant and just beginning to color. Add onions and salt, then stir together. Cover and cook, continuing to stir often and adjusting heat as necessary to prevent burning until soft and golden, about 10 to 15 minutes. Stir in tomato paste and oregano and cook, again stirring often, until the tomato paste has begun to brown on the bottom of the pan, about 2 to 4 minutes.

Pour in wine and vinegar. Reduce heat to a simmer and with a spoon, scrape up any browned particles on bottom of pot. Cook until slightly reduced, about 2 minutes. Add tomatoes and juice, then simmer for about 25 minutes, or until tomatoes are mostly broken down. Remove from heat. Add basil and pepper. Transfer sauce, in batches, to a blender or food processor (use caution when pureeing hot liquids), then process to desired consistency. For a smooth sauce, puree it all; for a chunky sauce, puree half and mix it back into the rest of the sauce.

Makes about six to eight cups

Vickie's Bars

This recipe from Jill Ross, owner of The Cookbook Stall, is a quick and easy dessert that can be prepared in less than an hour and is great for any last-minute guests. Jill learned to bake at her mother's side, and this recipe, one of her mother's favorites, is fondly named after her.

12 tablespoons (1½ sticks) butter
2¼ cups packed brown sugar
2½ cups all-purpose flour
2½ teaspoons baking powder

½ teaspoon baking soda
3 eggs
1 cup chocolate chips
1 cup chopped nuts, optional

Preheat oven to 350 degrees.

Grease a 15 × 10 × 1-inch baking pan.

In a saucepan, melt butter with packed brown sugar. Let cool for 10 minutes.

In a bowl, sift together flour, baking powder and baking soda.

In another bowl, beat eggs and stir into butter-sugar mixture. Add the flour mixture and mix well. Stir in chocolate chips and nuts, if using.

Spread mixture in prepared pan and bake for 25 to 30 minutes. Cool and cut into squares.

Makes about 12 squares

Index

Page numbers in bold refer to recipes.